Worshipping the Myths of

World War II

Also by Edward W. Wood, Jr.

On Being Wounded

Beyond the Weapons of Our Fathers

Worshipping the Myths of
World War II

Reflections on America's Dedication to War

EDWARD W. WOOD, JR.

Potomac Books, Inc.
Washington, D.C.

Permissions: See page 211

Library of Congress Cataloging-in-Publication Data

Wood, Edward W., Jr.
   Worshipping the myths of World War II : reflections on America's dedication to war / Edward W. Wood, Jr. — 1st ed.
      p. cm.
   Includes bibliographical references and index.
   ISBN 1-59797-016-6 (alk. paper)
      1. World War, 1939–1945—United States. 2. Collective memory—United States. 3. United States—Foreign relations—20th century. I. Title.

D769.1.W66 2006
940.53'73—dc22

                                        2006015432

ISBN 978-1-59797-163-8 (paperback)

Printed in the United States of America on acid-free paper that meets the American National Standards Institute Z39-48 Standard.

Potomac Books, Inc.
22841 Quicksilver Drive
Dulles, Virginia 20166

First Edition

10 9 8 7 6 5 4 3 2 1

DEDICATED

to the memories of
Glen Davis, Jr., and Byron Hedin,
killed in World War II,

and to

Bob Reed, Bill Montgomery, and
Ed Holmgren, who came home
from that war and struggled
to make our nation a better place

CONTENTS

~~~
PREFACE

Seriously wounded by artillery fire in the liberation of France from the Nazis in September 1944, I have struggled with the impacts of my injuries for over sixty years, always haunted by an irresolvable conflict. I knew on the one hand that the war had to be fought so as to preserve the nation and the democracy I so loved. This was the reason I had volunteered for line duty out of a safe college berth.

On the other hand, to the flesh and heart of me, I knew the horror of that war: the stark terror of combat; the wounds that changed my life forever; childhood friends killed or badly maimed; battle fatigue; the murderous destruction of English, German, and Japanese cities from the air; the shock of atomic weaponry; and the death of millions of innocent civilians, mostly women and children, in the Holocaust and the war's other atrocities. For long decades I lived with that conflict, remembering, with my other friends who served at the front, what that war was really like. I was saddened, then suddenly angry, as I watched the harsh reality of the war become softened, sweetened by what I came to recognize as the four Myths of World War II:

- The First Myth: "The Good War"
- The Second Myth: "The Greatest Generation"
- The Third Myth: "We Won World War II Largely on Our Own"
- The Fourth Myth: "When Evil Lies in Others, War Is the Means to Justice"

The impact of my wounds—I was hit by German shrapnel in head, buttock, pelvis, and suffered psychological wounds long before Post Traumatic Stress Disorder (PTSD) was identified—made it impossible for me to believe in these four myths that have masked the real nature of World War II and all our wars that followed. With increasing skepticism and contempt, I watched these myths mature, turning World War II into a time of national nobility, not the obscenity that I and most of the world experienced.

Those wounds and the emotions they engendered brought me irrevocably to this lifelong quest to understand the nature of war and these decades of wars and rumors of wars shadowing myself and my nation since our victory in 1945. In 1984, I returned to France and found the place of my wounding forty years before. That experience resulted in my first book, *On Being Wounded*, its first draft completed while I lived near the Cathedral of Chartres. A second book, *Beyond the Weapons of Our Fathers*, followed, exploring America's and my family's traditions of violence and war, as well as peace and compassion, over a three-hundred-year history.

America's dedication to war became even clearer to me when Tom Brokaw and Steven Ambrose first began to tell me that I was a member of a "Greatest Generation." I knew immediately that this was not true. I had done nothing great in World War II. I had simply done what I was supposed to do, my duty. My friends who had served in that war in combat felt the same. In fact, the phrase the "Greatest Generation" embarrassed us. I puzzled over the way the war's reality was glossed over by stories of heroism and stoicism under fire, avoiding what the war had really been like—its pain, suffering, betrayals, battle fatigue, desertions, deaths, woundings, and killings. I slowly began to realize as I read and re-read such writers as James Jones, Paul Fussell, and Howard Zinn that men needed to mask what they had really done in that war in order to hide the animals they had once been. Men turned the pain of their war into shining myths of courage, honor, comradeship, and glory.

Myth, according to Roland Barthes in Kevin Foster's *Fighting Fictions,* "is constituted by the loss of the historical quality of things: in it, things lose . . . memory. . . . Myth does not deny things, on the contrary . . . it purifies them, it makes them innocent, it gives them a natural and eternal justification, it gives them a clarity which is not that of an explanation but that of a statement of fact. . . . Myth acts economically: it abolishes the complexity of human acts."[1]

This definition of myth helped to clarify my understanding of America's dedication to war and formulate the four Myths of World War II presented in this book. Myth lets us mask the harsh difficulties of life we face, lets us lie about them, and turns ugliness into beauty and death into nobility. It purifies our memory.

My understanding of the four Myths of World War II occurred over many years. The first two myths—the "Good War" and the "Greatest Generation"—came easily, born from popular literature and film. Though the third myth—achieving victory alone—was also implicit in most popular literature, I discovered it most unexpectedly in many conversations about the war. Simply put, most people I talked with had only a vague idea of the contribution of the USSR to Allied victory and no memory of the role of China in the war. The fourth myth—war as the means to overcome evil—was built upon the significance of the Holocaust. The more I looked at what had happened to America over generations, the more I believed we have to understand our complicated relation to the Holocaust and the policies of appeasement and compromise it so soundly condemned. We need to understand the reasons the Holocaust is so profoundly important to our national thinking. It bred the deepest revulsion for acts of "Evil." That revulsion readied us to rush to acts of war against the latest evildoer, seldom considering alternatives.

Two men have accompanied me on my long search for the truths of war in America, as I tried to understand why we love war so much and why we believe that war inevitably leads to justice. Bob Reed lost his left hand as an infantryman in Leyte in 1944. Bill Montgomery was a stretcher-bearer who went across France and Germany with the Fourth Division in 1944 and 1945, winning three Bronze Stars. Bob, Bill, and I have been the closest of friends on our lifelong journey that began separately under fire in World War II. We first met at the University of Chicago immediately after our discharge, able to share our combat experience in the deepest of ways. Our friendship literally saved our lives, preventing, I am sure, the suicide of one of us. After retirement, we began to meet again once a year. In those grand nights and days of conversation, we talked of the war as it really was, contemptuous of its myths. All three of us were troubled by a terrible dilemma: we knew that World War II had to be fought and we were proud of our service, yet we loathed the war and the barbarism we had experienced.

From this lifetime of friendship and that terrible paradox, much of this book was nourished. An extension of my earlier two efforts that were written before our current war in Iraq, this present book pushes ahead the ideas developed then, applying them to this newest of America's wars, the "War on Terror." It searches for uncomfortable truths about America's national character that lie behind both our enthusiastic acceptance of war and our propensity for war-making since our victory in 1945. For over sixty years, troops and innocent civilians have been killed and wounded in Korea, Vietnam, Lebanon, Grenada, Panama, Somalia, the Persian Gulf, and now Afghanistan and Iraq. In that time, we supported warlike and authoritarian regimes throughout the world and continue that assistance today in such nations as Saudi Arabia. We have troops stationed in sixty-two countries.[2] Our military budget, euphemistically called a defense budget, is by far the largest in the world, as if we cannot manage a national existence without a war and an "enemy" to define us and without a steady escalation of our war-making capacity.[3] Nine years before 9/11, a year after the Gulf War, our current vice president, Dick Cheney, predicted the continuation of war as an American reality, even though there was no known enemy at that time. He said in 1992: "We are arguing that there will be a time again when U.S. military forces are likely to be required."[4]

He has certainly fulfilled his prediction. War has become a central occupation of America.

Historians such as Robert Gildea in *Marianne in Chains* and W. G. Sebald in *On the Natural History of Destruction* now demand a reconsideration of the events of World War II in France and Germany.[5] For too long, we in the United States have masked our actions in that war with the Myths of World War II.

I hope this book will bring us closer to the terrible truths of World War II that lie behind those myths. I hope it will help us reevaluate America's role in that war, help clear away its myths so that, at last, we can see war's destructive cruelty with far greater clarity. I hope that reevaluation will help us think more clearly about our struggles with terrorism in this new millennium, rather than continue to think we can vanquish terrorists only through acts of war and violence, excluding more gentle policies.

~∾~

In writing and developing this book, I wish to acknowledge so much help. I know I stand on the shoulders of giants. I would particularly like to thank Howard Zinn, whose support for *Beyond the Weapons of My Fathers* was carried forward in his help in finding a publisher for this present book. His personal life, kindness, and brilliance remain an inspiration. Jack Hall first supported my work, and his daughter, Noa Hall, brought *Beyond the Weapons of My Fathers* to Howard Zinn's attention. Paul Fussell gave me an endorsement for *On Being Wounded*, and his books have blazed the way for this effort. He is remarkable in his understanding of all war has done to America, England, and the rest of the world, and in his ability to present his discoveries in moving prose. I consider the late James Jones's trilogy, *From Here to Eternity, The Thin Red Line,* and *Whistle*, to be the most profound fiction of World War II. It has helped me enormously in seeing the reality of my war.

John McCamant's consistent and wise advice has been immeasurable in pushing the boundaries of my work. He particularly supported me in the critical re-reading of the final draft. Our lunches remain a moment of sanity in an increasingly difficult world. Pat Frederick, the editor of my first book, *On Being Wounded,* picked its manuscript out of the pile. Her editing skills made great improvements. Before that, John Williams and Richard McDonough had made real efforts to bring it to publication. Bob Baron, the publisher of my first two books, and the editor of my last, has been a support beyond the telling of it. Henry Sauerwein, Jr., of the Wurlitzer Foundation, dead these many years, will always be a treasured memory for his critical thinking. Donald Anderson, editor of *War, Literature, & the Arts* at the USAF Academy, has been of real assistance, a thoughtful man, and it is with his kind permission that I based chapter four on an article I wrote for his fine publication. Paula Van Dusen kept the computer and printer going. Dan MacMeekin read the first draft and recommended that Potomac give the manuscript serious consideration, for which I am deeply grateful. Don McKeon of Potomac Books, Inc., accepted his recommendation and since then has put me through the wringer in so many helpful ways—a real gentleman with a wonderful eye. His staff has provided the same level of aid. My readers—Dean Baxter, Jay Balzer, Joan Lidell, David Poundstone, Tom Rauch, David Van Meter, and Nancy Wood—were of the most enormous help in leading me into new insights about this effort. Nancy's insight into the hard task of writing remains of greatest help. Sasha Chachavadze, Naomi Horii, Nell Husted, Siena Sanderson, and Phil Woods have always given great support. Personnel at the Denver Public Library in both the reference and magazine departments have given real service in tracking down those sources always so difficult to find, especially at the end of manuscript preparation. And without the advice, daily assistance, support, criticism, and review of Elaine Granata, this book would never have been completed.

INTRODUCTION

Worshipping War in America

The thing I find most puzzling about the United States today is how little real debate there has been over the almost unanimous acceptance of the idea that the only way to defeat terrorism is through policies of war and violence and that "Good" will always come from armed conflict. Though lip service may be given to additional policies such as law enforcement, and may sometimes involve a discussion of causes of terrorism, ranging from the poverty of Third World nations to the virulence of fundamentalist Muslim beliefs, energy has almost totally been devoted to strategies of war and acts of revenge: the defeat of the Taliban in Afghanistan, followed by a moral failure to clean up the mess we have made; the policy of preemption, adopted in the war with Iraq and its tragic failure, leading to a moral and physical abyss for our soldiers and Iraqi citizens, suffering and pain common to both; the rise in the defense budget and the concomitant decline in domestic spending; the formation of a Federal Department of Homeland Security; the collection of all data available on every foreigner in America so that terrorists can be readily tracked; the proposed collection of data on every American for that same

reason; the steady erosion of civil liberties, particularly for Muslims; the rise in hate crimes against
Muslims; our easy application of torture to suspected
terrorists and the use of the concentration camp
without rule of law for those terrorists.

In 2003 eighty percent of Americans believed
that war may lead to justice. And our military remains our most revered institution.[1]

This book points to the unstudied and forgotten reality that these beliefs, strategies, and tactics,
central to our foreign policy since World War II and
exacerbated following 9/11, are rooted in a past
running on toward sixty years—the way World War
II and its myths are remembered in America. Our
stunning victory over the Germans and our liberation of their concentration camps, followed quickly
by the use of the atomic bomb and the defeat of the
Japanese in 1945, fixed into our minds the beliefs
that war was the best, the only means for destroying "Evil," and that appeasement or compromise
would always lead to disaster. Our brilliant triumph
over the USSR in the Cold War but carried forward
this certainty in American ability to win in any war
and, so, expand American hegemony over the globe.
The defeat in Vietnam was but a "blip" on our over-
all rise to international dominance that began with
our victory in World War II.

How did we fall into this pattern of accepting
war as the central means for solving international
problems, miring ourselves in Third World nations
from Vietnam to Afghanistan and Iraq, arming ourselves with such powerful weapons and basing our
power on those weapons, turning not only rogue
states but much of the world so bitterly against us?
How did we come to accept what President
Eisenhower so aptly called "the military-industrial
complex" as essential to our way of life? By the end

of the Vietnam War—in fact into the 1980s—military solutions to international policy were largely seen as failures by the United States, the danger of another Vietnam. For a few short years, the use of the military as a way to solve our relations with the remainder of the world was simply forbidden. We had failed so miserably in Vietnam that the use of American force seemed a path to more failure.

But, in a series of decisions beginning in the early 1980s, exploding at the end of that decade, continuing into the 1990s, and now into this third millennium, that posture has seemingly been irrevocably reversed. In October of 1983, 241 Marine and Navy personnel were killed in Lebanon by a terrorist attack. Two days later President Ronald Reagan ordered the invasion of Grenada. At the same time his administration continued the support of repressive Central American governments. The Iran-Contra affair occurred in 1985–1986. In 1989 we invaded Panama; in the early winter of 1991 came the Gulf War; in the late fall of 1993 the pitched battle in Somalia, resulting in our retreat from that country; at the end of the Clinton administration we used force in the former Yugoslavia, ending with our bombing of Serbia.[2]

At the same moment—and this is where the timing seems so exquisite—our worship of World War II as the apogee of the nation's greatest honor, glory, and patriotism simply exploded in all forms of media. The resurgence began in 1984, with the publication of Studs Terkel's *The Good War.* On the fortieth Anniversary of D-Day, that same year, President Reagan went to the beachhead and praised the "boys of Pointe-du-Hoc." Remembrance escalated in the 1990s with the work of Steven Ambrose extolling the bravery of the "Citizen Soldier" on D-Day and in the battle for Europe, followed by Tom Brokaw's

"Greatest Generation" and Steven Spielberg's movie *Saving Private Ryan*. World War II evolved into a warm and fuzzy glow when American soldiers were giants, heroic, stoical, and always true to their country and the cause of freedom. War was the means to give America power and spread its message over the world: war was "Good," fought by the "Greatest Generation," which was able to crush "Evil" largely on its own, without allies—the accomplishments of England, the USSR, and China neglected. Our worship of World War II culminated in the proposal to build its memorial on the Mall in Washington; now completed. Its opening on Memorial Day weekend, 2004, was a national TV event.

After the terrorist attack on 9/11 war worship took another turn with a new generation of war lovers, exemplified by the work of Victor Davis Hanson and Max Boot. Hanson in *An Autumn of War* wrote: "War—whether to end slavery, to ruin the Nazi death camps, or to dismantle the Japanese military—has in fact ended great evil inflicted on millions." Further back in American history he admires Sherman's march through Georgia, its destruction of infrastructure and civilian support for the war: "In the present context, [2001] General Sherman would advise our military planners to use crushing force against our enemies in the Middle East, targeted especially against those who started the war, the personal assets of the terrorists, and the government and military infrastructure of the Taliban and Iraq."[3]

Max Boot writes: "Since the fall of the Berlin Wall, America has stood head and shoulders (and also probably torso) above all other nations, possessor of the world's richest economy and its most potent military . . . the United States thrust willy-nilly into Britain's old role as globocop. . . . Africa, the Middle East, Central Asia, the Balkans, and other regions teeming with failed states, criminal states, or simply a state of nature. . . . America has found itself getting involved in its recent small wars, and no doubt will again in the future."[4]

Scott Simon of National Public Radio, expressing what was then the will of 90 percent of Americans, wrote in a Commentary in the *Wall Street Journal* in October, 2001: "American pacifists have no sane alternative now but to support war. . . . Only American (and British) power can stop more killing in the world's skyscrapers, pizza parlors, embassies, bus stations, ships, and airplanes."[5]

The most striking unity in all these proclamations is the certainty that massive war—destruction of the enemy's military force and infrastructure, unconditional surrender, domination of its people—is the path, the one true path, to stop "Evil" and to protect and spread freedom and, now, to prevent terrorism. There are no unforeseen consequences in this scenario, no downsides, no comprehension of the death and wounding of our soldiers and of thousands of innocent civilians, mostly women and children, no recognition of the destruction of towns and cities, the infrastructure that makes civilization possible. War, mighty war, seizes our imagination and becomes the instantaneous solution to our problems. In patriotic fervor, Congress cedes the war power to the president, whether in Vietnam or in Iraq.

This frame of public, media, literary, and academic support for war and our war against terrorism, rising out of the memory of a cleaned-up World War II, served our political leaders very well in their actions following September 11, 2001. The president, in a Memorial Day speech in 2002 in France celebrating D-Day, compared World War II to the campaign against terrorism.[6] In a visit to Auschwitz, on May 31, 2003, he said, "All the good that has come to this [European] continent—all the progress, the prosperity, the peace—came because beyond the barbed wire there were people willing to take up arms against evil."[7]

Vice President Dick Cheney, Secretary of Defense Donald Rumsfeld, and his former assistant, Paul Wolfowitz, all share this belief that the way to defeat terrorists, their "Evil" in Iraq, Afghanistan, and other "rogue states," is through the threat or the use of the war power. These beliefs and actions are modeled on our stunning success in World War II. Condoleezza Rice, previously national security advisor, now secretary of state, uses the model of World War II in a different way by praising the North Atlantic Treaty Organization (NATO) and the Marshall Plan through which America provided resources to rehabilitate defeated nations after our World War II victory. She sees the upside of that war, the new world of democracy and freedom built out of its shambles, as an example for American efforts in the Middle East that emphasize "the spread of [democratic] . . . values that will make us more secure."[8]

The Bush administration's views on the efficacy of war are well represented in the *National Security Strategy* it issued in the fall of 2002.[9] That document moves beyond self-defense to the policy of preemption, the right to make a unilateral military attack on some other nation if we believe that at some undefined time in the future that nation might challenge America's security. The result: U.S. foreign policy now endorses war at will as we please on whom we please. That policy was first implemented in March of 2003 when the United States, Britain, and its coalition attacked Iraq without the United Nations' approval and over the bitter disagreement of France, Germany, and Russia. The philosophy of the way to fight terrorism or to halt rogue states from possessing the atomic bomb rests squarely on the four Myths of World War II presented in the Preface. War becomes a form of American triumphalism, the certainty that we have the answers to the problems of the world and have the right to impose our answers upon all nations of that world.

Not one of the men and women in the administration who so praise war and its positive consequences has ever been in war. (In fact, the vice president and the secretary of defense assiduously avoided service in the Vietnam War, while the president skipped combat by serving in the Texas Air National Guard). Not one of them has ever discussed in public—and I would hazard a guess in private— the unintended costs of war, even after more than three disastrous years in Iraq. Imagination forms their wars, images that must be drawn from movies, books, and memoirs, images that never convey war's reality. The president sees war in his public speeches as the way to eradicate evil. He expected the war in Iraq to be one of liberation, its people welcoming our troops. He never expected that some of our soldiers would commit barbaric atrocities that would shatter our moral image in the world and turn many Muslims and citizens of other nations more deeply against us. Neither he nor his advisors have apparently ever wrestled with the meaning of Aeschylus's *The Persians* or *The Oresteia,* Euripides' *The Trojan Women,* and Thucydides' *History of the Peloponnesian War,* plays and histories showing how hubris, pride, and arrogance destroyed the Athenians. They do not understand the unintended consequences of war when undertaken by a powerful nation, particularly how the destruction of innocents breeds hatred and how that hatred can destroy even the greatest power.

These men and women in the administration

define the nations and peoples of the world as "Good" and "Evil." We represent the forces of good. Saddam Hussein in Iraq came quickly to symbolize the power of evil. President Bush and his associates characterized Hussein as the dark enemy, possessed with super-human qualities. Though Iraq was strapped financially by sanctions for twelve years, the administration still believed Hussein possessed the ability to create all kinds of weapons of mass destruction, from chemical to biological to nuclear bombs. In response to our removing Hussein from power, President Bush and his advisors expected the people of Iraq to rise in unison and greet American forces with open and loving arms, as the citizens of Europe did in the summer and fall of 1944. The administration never bothered to think about the impact of actions that killed innocent women and children in a society where family and clan are so important; they never bothered to understand that the Shiites had already been twice attacked by the West—once in the 1920s by the British, who bombed helpless villagers; and once in the 1990s when the first President Bush encouraged them to rise, then deserted them, leaving them helpless before the repressive rage of the then-President Hussein.[10] They apparently never bothered to study the formation of Iraq after World War I, when three incompatible peoples—the Sunnis, Shiites, and Kurds—were thrown together as a nation, a patch-work quilt of tribes that had distrusted each other for centuries.[11] Most of all they never bothered to understand that war, once entered, becomes a cauldron, a series of uncontrolled events, events that can turn on the perpetrators and strike with the ferocity of a rattle-snake. The images of war that blinded President Bush and his advisors must have been composed of snatches of a thousand movies and television spectaculars: John Wayne in *Sands of Iwo Jima*; Tom Hanks leading his valiant warriors to the beaches and into the *bocage* of Normandy to find Private Ryan; Audie Murphy winning his Congressional Medal of Honor.

It was their turn now—the president, administration, and many in Congress. They would have their "Good War." They would become another Great Generation. They would conquer "Evil" with "Good," free a repressed population, bring democracy and free markets to thirsting nations, turn the Middle East into a replica of the western world, then, using Iraq as an example, free the other nations of the Middle East, and, finally, pacify the warring Israelis and Palestinians. They would reach these goals through war and the mighty force of arms, making war the means to moral purity. They never understood the down side of war as those of us did who fought at the front: war is a dirty, nasty business of killing and breaking things that corrupts those who fight it.

The debate about the war carried on in the presidential election of 2004 and now in this winter of 2005–2006 it seldom criticizes the assumptions of the current administration that war is a "Good," the only way to eradicate "Evil." Critics of the war in Iraq center on the failure to discover weapons of mass destruction, on the failure to deal adequately with bin Laden, al Qaeda, and al-Zarqawi, on the bypassing of the United Nations, on the size, arming, and morale of our troops, and on prison atrocities. They emphasize training Iraqi troops, determining an exit policy, and casualties. They decry the fact that it is mostly the poor and minorities who are fighting our war in Iraq. They almost never question the assumption that war is an inevitable good, with no downsides. Some "liberal" leaders, such as Senator Hillary Clinton, even emphasize that we need more troops.[12] They seldom demand that we take a hard look at ourselves, asking why we are so hated and what we do to cause that hate. They seldom raise other fundamental questions: what are the causes of terrorism? Does war against states ever bring to justice individuals who commit terrorist acts? Rather, are some new forms of action required, some new ways of thinking about the means the United States should use to oppose terrorism? Is law enforcement a better option than war? They rarely question the size and scope of the Defense Department budget, which rises inexorably each year.

With the enormous military power the United States now possesses, far exceeding that of any other nation or grouping of nations in world history, combined with the fact that we can kill so easily at a distance without even disturbing our daily routine, it is at last time for our policy makers—and ourselves, as citizens—to ask what war really means, its true costs, its true impact upon both ourselves and the world. Is it the right policy, is it the only policy for rooting out a terrible disease, the terrorist murder of innocents? Do we really understand what we are doing when we commit the nation to a war on terrorism?

The last time civilians in America had direct contact with war's brutality in the continental United States (except for Pancho Villa's raid on Columbus, New Mexico in 1916) was in the Civil War, nearly a hundred and fifty years ago. In spite of the horrific event of 9/11, when it comes to war we still are a nation that revels in myth and fantasy. Most of all at this time in our history, before we continue our plunge into preemptive repression of terrorists in states other than Iraq or attacks on nations whom we believe verge on possession of atomic weaponry such as Iran or North Korea, it is essential that we pause for a moment in this struggle to understand all that such acts of "war" actually entail. Is war the best means to pursue our self-interest in this new kind of struggle with single and savage individuals willing to die as long as they destroy those they call "infidels?" Does war only enflame them to commit even more barbaric suicide bombings? Before we in America can ever construct a useful foreign policy and stop our ceaseless forays into misadventures in Third World countries from Korea to Vietnam to Iraq as we have over the past fifty-plus year period, we need, most of all, to look with a hard eye at the nature of war and our inheritance of the myths of war from World War II, where our faith in the goodness of war began.

We so easily forget that, in the 1930s, after the horror of the trench warfare of World War I and in the midst of the Great Depression, many in the United States reviled both war and the military. In April of 1935, "60,000 college students around the nation went on strike against war. The next November, 20,000 students in New York marched in the streets."[13] There were attacks on war from movies like *All Quiet on the Western Front* and novels like Dalton Trumbo's *Johnny Got His Gun* and Hemingway's *Farewell to Arms.* In fact, in 1939 our army was one of the smallest in the "civilized" world, with only one hundred and ninety thousand men.[14] Members of that army were mocked by writers such as Thomas Wolfe, who wrote of: "the cheap, tough, and slovenly appearance of a private soldier in the United States Army."[15] We so easily forget that World War II never touched the continental United States, except for one light shelling by a Japanese submarine on the coast of California.[16] For the rest of the world, for those of us who fought it on the ground or in the air, for those of other nations who suffered

barbaric combat casualties, who lived under ceaseless bombing attacks, died in concentration camps
and military prisons, it was a time of enormous pain
and suffering. How could it be good, how could those
who fought it and perpetrated such acts be great?

America needs to ask questions it has not asked
for these many decades: can freedom, justice, and
democracy ever come from the barrel of a gun? It is
time to examine our whole war-making system,
beginning with the enormous and bloated Department of Defense that has been erected on the memories of World War II and all our wars since. It is time
to examine the policy of preemption that now guides
our foreign policy. It is time to ask what our dedication to war as the means to justice has actually done
to the nation and the world, with the past sixty years
of draws and defeats in our sallies into Third World
nations, with the killing and wounding of around
four hundred thousand of our young men and
women in our armed forces since 1945, with the killing and wounding of millions of innocents in Third
World nations all over the globe.[17] We must unravel
the great many myths and fantasies about the reality of war we have accumulated since our victory at
the end of World War II, most of all the belief that in
the "Good War," fought by the "Greatest Generation," Americans achieved a stunning victory against
"Evil," without great costs and largely without Allied aid. War has become in our minds and culture
the means to justice, the only way to stop terrorists
and other men and women of violence. We must
now question how these myths have led us to an
easy acceptance of war, always willing to support
it in the general public, vote for it in Congress, and
give the executive branch the right to fight a war as
it pleases.

A hard look at these myths is the purpose of

this slim book. In chapters one through nine, it scrutinizes the four Myths of World War II, describing what World War II was really like:

● The First Myth: "The Good War" is belied by the killing of innocents, by the nature of killing in World War II, and by what really happened to many of us hurt in combat.

● The Second Myth: "The Greatest Generation" is disproved by the reality behind the war movie, memoir, and novel; the discussion shows how the generation that fought the war also helped defeat the hope for peace that swept the world at the end of World War II.

● The Third Myth: "We Won the War Largely on Our Own" is discussed in all its complexity. The war would not have been won without our massive production of goods and matériel as the arsenal of democracy, our will for victory, and the battle skills and sacrifices of our troops. At the same time, we often tend to neglect the enormous contributions of Britain, the USSR, and China with a far longer war, far higher casualties, soldier and civilian, and, often, obliteration of their urban and natural environment. The popular mind ignores these burdens carried by other nations, holding to the simplistic myth of winning on our own.

● The Fourth Myth: "When Evil Lies in Others, War Is the Means to Justice," a belief inherited from World War II and its Holocaust, is questioned, as is the notion that compro-

mise and cooperation are always appeasement. Only war is the solution to those regimes that make atrocities or threaten world
peace, claims this myth. The inheritance from
World War I that laid the foundation for World
War II and its Holocaust is also examined.

Chapter ten, the conclusion, contains a message of sanity, I believe, of returning to those years
immediately after World War II before the myths of
the "Good War" were formed and masked the real
nature of that war, that moment from 1945 to 1946
when the world hesitated on the cusp of a new way
of life. Out of the pain of World War II, we who had
fought it and been so hurt in it dreamed that a new
world might be born, the secret of the atomic bomb
shared, steps toward world cooperation taken, ideas
about a more equitable distribution of the world's
goods approached, ways of policing insurgents in
terms of international law and international action
developed. Though these hopes have been lost—
even mocked—for over fifty years, perhaps they can
now be reborn, combined with the knowledge the
world has gained from fifty years of war and suffering and abortive efforts for world peace. Even more
important, perhaps the United States can, at last,
rediscover its true role as the leader of a revived
movement toward a peaceful world. Suggestions for
new beginnings—new ways of thinking and acting—
are required, ways to imagine a world without those
myths. We need to be able to think about that new
world, what it might be; we need to act to achieve
it. New leaders will be needed, bold enough to break
the chains of our sixty year dedication to the Myths
of World War II and the wars they breed.

Most of us understand that our unconscious governs many of our actions. We often mask the harshest of realities with words that veil our real motivations. The myths examined in this book contain those beliefs that have given us the permission to make war in so many places over sixty years, myths we accept that let us deny the hard truth of our wars.

Though we have many images of these sixty years, perhaps the essential one is our enormous and overflowing cornucopia of material goods, shown on television every night, presented in every glossy magazine, available in a thousand malls, the goods for which we are told to live.

Yet, for me, there are other images that tell the true tale of those sixty-plus years since the end of World War II. In the last scene of the movie *The Bridges of Toko-Ri*, a tale of the Korean War, two pilots, played by William Holden and Mickey Rooney, have been shot down over North Korea. Alive, they have only small arms for protection. In the distance Chinese and North Korean troops move toward them. Their death is inevitable. They are alone, forgotten by America. A still photograph taken in the War in Vietnam shows a frightened and naked girl fleeing toward the camera, escaping the terror and pain of bombing from napalm. In another photograph a Vietnamese police chief shoots an unarmed man in the head with his pistol. In Iraq American soldiers, male and female, torture and humiliate Iraqi prisoners.

These images, to me, represent the central symbols of our time, lying beneath our cornucopia of material goods, the world we have made of war. Our young men and women fight our wars in dirty little ditches, harassed by foreign soldiers they cannot understand, certain to die for causes they do not grasp. Millions of innocent civilians are killed or injured by our bombers and prisoners are tortured and killed by our soldiers and the mercenaries we hire. Meanwhile the American public believes these myths of war that deny war's reality and revels in its marketplace, either totally ignorant of or carelessly denying our warring actions over the earth.

Our first step in breaking America's dedication to war is to recognize how linked we are to the four Myths of World War II. And that is the purpose of this book, to help us understand those myths so we can transcend them and adopt new ways of thinking and acting.

Part I

The First Myth:
"The Good War"

CHAPTER 1

The Killing of Innocents

Where did the idea of a "Good War" come from? How could there possibly ever be a "Good War?" I first heard World War II referred to as such in the 1980s with Studs Terkel's book by that name. He wrote, "The title of this book was suggested by Herb Mitgang, who experienced World War II as an army correspondent. It is a phrase that has been frequently voiced by men of his and my generation."[1]

My own fierce conviction is that this judgment of World War II is held predominantly by those who have only read about the war in popular literature or seen it in popular movies, observed it as correspondents, written about it without experiencing combat as a soldier, sat it out behind the front, or grown fat with it in an America untouched by war's disaster. Those who lost family members or were unfortunate enough to be Japanese or other minorities, and particularly those of us who fought that war, quickly learned that World War II was about one thing and one thing only: killing. It was not wholly about defending the nation, though that was one of its stated goals; it was not wholly about making the world safe for Roosevelt and Churchill's Four Freedoms though that, too, was part of its goal.

It was about killing Germans, Japanese, and Italians—soldiers and civilians—men, women, and children. It was about the killing of innocents. It was about the unconditional surrender of our enemies.

From September 1, 1939, to August 14, 1945, we and our Allies killed an estimated six to eight million German, Japanese, and Italian soldiers, sailors, airmen, and marines. The Allied forces lost at least fourteen million armed personnel, largely Russian and Chinese. In addition, probably three times that number were wounded, many maimed for life. Around three hundred thousand of those killed and seven hundred thousand of those wounded were American, a minuscule proportion of the total number lost by the Allies.[2]

But these figures are small when compared to civilian casualties, a total we will never really know, estimated from fifty to sixty million killed, twelve million in the "concentration camp and slave labor system."[3] The world became accustomed to the killing of innocents in massive numbers in that war. This killing of innocents occurred in so many offensive ways, on the ground by gunshot, club, carbon monoxide, and the gas Zyklon B, but much of it occurred from the air from English and American bombers. Such killing was totally unknown to Americans who are largely acquainted with the fact of killing in war only through movies, television, radio, and newspapers. But these media, which at their very best relay little of the real experience of combat, lie. They never expose, most of all, the defecations and urinations that stain a dying body, the sweet and sick smell of blood that settles so heavily on the air and in the nostrils, the flies that blacken wounds while body parts and gore dirty the earth. This is the reality that must be understood about World War II. It was not good; it was a time of killing, wounding, and injuring men and women and children all over the globe. We have hundreds of movies of our soldiers in combat in that war; we have few of the women and children killed from the air.

And this is the purpose of this part of this book: to look at World War II as it really was, not as our politicians have named it, not as a new generation of movie-makers, writers, TV producers, directors and actors have imagined it, none of whom ever experienced that war as it really was, never "Good" but a time of barbarism.

~~~

World War II improved on two methods for the mass killing of innocent civilians developed in earlier wars. It turned these techniques into the most sophisticated ways of killing ever known to humanity. The first came on the ground in the German killing of Jews, Poles, Russians, so-called "undesirables" such as the mentally handicapped, Gypsies, homosexuals, priests and ministers, members of the Resistance, and prisoners of war. It came as well with the Japanese rape of Nanking and Shanghai and the occupation of Korea, where the total number of persons killed is unknown; and with the Russian willingness to murder Polish officers, leave the partisans in Warsaw to lose their rebellion, kill and rape German civilians, and let their German prisoners of war die through starvation and sickness. Killing on the ground occurred in all kinds of ways: a pistol shot to the back of the neck; machine guns mowing down helpless civilians; trucks pouring carbon monoxide into locked compartments; starvation; Zyklon B drifting into locked shower rooms; the sword and axe slicing heads from bodies; the fist beating members of the Resistance to death; soldiers raping women until they died, shoving broom handles far up soft vaginas; cutting a fetus from a woman's womb, killing it.

The second effort at killing came from the air. Its roots were in World War I when German dirigibles bombed London. It continued in the 1920s when the British bombed Shiites in Iraq, in 1935–36 when Mussolini's Italian air force bombed Ethiopians, and from 1936 to 1939, when the Spanish Fascists—and the planes of Nazi Germany—bombed and destroyed the cities of Loyalist Spaniards. But those were only preliminaries to what became a kind of killing as despicable as that of the concentration camp. Hitler started it in 1940 with the dive-bombing of Holland, then bombing and strafing French civilians fleeing Paris, and continued it that same fall in such cities as London and Liverpool, with an estimated sixty thousand civilians killed in England alone.[4] Killing from the air expanded greatly with the Allied bombing of Hamburg, Dresden, then Berlin; sixty-one German cities in all demolished (and some put this figure as high as 131) and six hundred thousand German civilians killed. Cities were destroyed and civilians killed throughout Europe, as well. The bombings in Japan killed one hundred thousand in one night in Tokyo. The bombings concluded with dropping the atomic bombs on Hiroshima and Nagasaki, where over one hundred thousand were killed outright; the numbers wounded and scarred for life are uncertain.[5]

Little concern has ever been given to linking these two kinds of killing in WWII, one on the ground, and the other from the air. In the popular mind the Holocaust on the ground and the war from the air possess different qualities. The one on the ground is offensive in nature because men killed innocents directly, women and children especially, while the killing in the air war is imbued with some purity, almost as if the killing came from God.

Yet by treating them as opposite ends of the same reality, the killing of innocents, it is perhaps possible to learn a little more about the quality of the world we inherited from the defeat of the Germans and the Japanese by the Allies in 1945. It is this fact of killing of innocents in numbers so great they can scarcely be imagined that links the major combatant nations of World War II: Japan, Germany, the USSR, England, and the United States. It is, perhaps, the essential characteristic of that war that so distinguishes it from all other wars. Three of these nations—Japan, Germany, and the USSR—were in the business of killing innocents directly, face to face, and also by air. Two did it largely by air: England and the United States.

In Germany, the men of Reserve Police Battalion 101, as reported in the book *Ordinary Men* by Christopher R. Browning, were responsible for the slaughter of great numbers of Jews by fist, bullet, and fire in Poland in 1942, slaughter done mercilessly by some, regretfully by others, with only a few refusing that duty.[6] SS members of the *Einsatzgruppen* began a continuous murder of Jews, Poles, and Russians, again face to face, in 1941, and carried it ahead in 1942 and 1943, while other soldiers in the SS ran the concentration camp system.[7] In the USSR advance toward Germany, rape and murder of German civilians were also common, retaliation for the terrible brutality of the German army. "Of a total of 3,060,000 German soldiers who had been taken prisoner by the Soviets, 1,094,250 died or lost their lives in other ways."[8] In 1937, as reported in *The Rape of Nanking* by Iris Chang, Japanese soldiers ran amok for weeks, killing Chinese prisoners, raping Chinese women, then killing them and murdering their babies. A favorite method of killing was beheading.[9]

From 1942 to 1945 English and American bombers wasted Germany and its people, Hamburg and Dresden totally flattened, people killed by firestorms. In Hamburg in the hot summer of 1943 so many swarms of fat bluebottle flies fed on corpses buried in the rubble that the city became almost uninhabitable. *Under the Bombs* provides this vivid description:

> Death laid grisly upon thousands of Hamburgers during this night. Some died softly, smothered by carbon monoxide within air-raid shelters. Some died in agony, caught in the streets as the fires raged like banshees among the fleeing. Women found the thin summer dresses they wore aflame and tore them off as they ran. Some of them stumbled alive into the air-raid shelters—a completely naked woman in the advanced stages of pregnancy lurched through the door of one of the main fire department shelters and shortly afterwards delivered her child in the bunker. Other naked women lay among the dead on the streets, seemingly untouched by the flames but dying from the effects of the excessive heat. There were stories of the shrinking and mummification of those who died.[10]

Firestorms in Japanese cities lit by American B-29 bombers in the spring of 1945 killed hundreds of thousands of Japanese. Holocausts from the air, the atomic bombs dropped by American B-29s, ended the war with the incomprehensible destruction of Hiroshima and Nagasaki.

Perhaps the essential similarity of all these actions is best portrayed by simply quoting descriptions of some of them, beginning with a Japanese soldier remembering the rape of Nanking in China years later. From *The Rape of Nanking*: "Few knew that soldiers impaled babies on bayonets and tossed them still alive into pots of boiling water. They gang-raped women from the ages of twelve to eighty and then killed them when they could no longer satisfy sexual requirements. I beheaded people, starved them to death, burned them, and buried them alive, over two hundred in all. It is terrible that I could turn into an animal and do these things. There are really no words to explain what I was doing. I was truly a devil."[11]

And, as reported in *The Making of the Atomic Bomb* by Richard Rhodes, the opposite end of killing technology, done safely from the air in the atomic bombing of Hiroshima, is described:

> The temperature at the site of the explosion . . . reached [5,400° F] . . . and primary atomic bomb thermal injury . . . was found in those exposed within [2 miles] of the hypocenter. . . . Primary burns are injuries of a special nature and not ordinarily experienced in everyday life. . . . Ah, that instant! I felt as though I had been struck on the back with something like a big hammer, and thrown into boiling oil. . . . I seem to have been blown a good way to the north, and I felt as though the directions were all changed around. . . . The vicinity was in pitch darkness; from the depths of the gloom, bright red flames rise crackling, and spread moment by moment. The faces of my friends who just before were working energetically are now burned and

blistered, their clothes torn to rags; to what shall I liken their trembling appearance as they stagger about? . . . The appearance of people was . . . well, they all had skin blackened by burns. . . . They had no hair because their hair was burned, and at a glance you couldn't tell whether you were looking at them from in front or in back. . . . They held their arms [in front of them] . . . and their skin—not only on their hands, but on their faces and bodies too—hung down.[12]

How little such reports differ from all the terrible descriptions of the camps of the German Holocaust as described by Konnilyn G. Feig in *Hitler's Death Camps*:

Through many sleepless nights I had been haunted by the tragic contrast between the beautiful beds of flowers and the crime-soaked atmosphere of the camp. Often when I reflected on the loving care which the Gestapo butchers lavished on these flower beds, I thought I would lose my mind. In this place where the most cold-blooded murderers studied and practiced the murder of human beings, flowers were cherished and kept alive with the greatest affection. . . .The gas squads packed the 2000 victims into the room. From the ceiling hung imitation shower heads. The doors were closed, the air was pumped out, and the gas poured in. . . . While the victims were dying the SS watched through the peepholes. When they opened the doors, they found the victims in half-sitting positions in a towerlike pile. Most were pink, others were covered with green spots. Some had foam on their lips, while others were bleeding at the nose. Many had their eyes open. The majority was packed near the doors . . . pit burning became the chief method of corpse disposal . . . [as described by a witness]. The corpses in the pit looked as if they had been chained together. Tongues of a thousand tiny blue-red flames were licking at them. The fire grew fiercer and flames leapt higher and higher. Under the ever-increasing heat a few of the dead began to stir, writhing as though with some unbearable pain, arms and legs straining in slow motion, and even their bodies straightening up a little, hesitant and with difficulty, almost as if with their last strength they were trying to rebel against their doom.[13]

A similar scene of horror followed the firebombing in Tokyo. From *The Rising Sun* by John Toland:

The [American] pathfinders had not yet been discovered in their low sweep toward the unwary city at better than 300 miles an hour. The first two planes . . . released their string of bombs in perfect unison at 12:15 A.M. [March 10, 1945]. One hundred feet above the ground the M47 missiles split apart, scattering two-foot-long napalm sticks which burst into flame on impact, spreading jellied fire. . . .Ten more pathfinders roared in to drop their napalm. . . . Then came the main force . . . at altitudes varying from of 4,900 to 9,200 feet. . . . Whipped by a stiffening wind, the fires spread rapidly. . . . Huge balls of fire leaped from building to building with hurricane force, creating an incandescent tidal wave exceeding 1,800 degrees Fahrenheit. . . . The center of Tokyo was as incandescent as the sun. . . . Thousands crouched terrified in their wooden shelters where they would be roasted alive. . . . The tremendous thermals of heat buffeted the B-29s overhead, tossing some of them several thousand feet upward in the air. Far above, the plane carrying [U.S. General in charge] LeMay's chief of staff, Brigadier General Thomas Powers, cruised back and forth. He photographed the conflagration, and reported to LeMay that Tokyo was an inferno. The crews in the last waves could smell the stench of burned flesh; some men vomited.[14]

The same scene had been replayed earlier over Hamburg, Dresden, Berlin, so many cities in Europe, beginning in 1942.

Gen. Curtis LeMay, Jr., one of the leaders of the air raids in Europe before taking command of the B-29s in the South Pacific in 1945, said, "I'll tell you what war is about—you've got to kill people, and when you've killed enough they stop fighting."[15] He recognized, however, "I suppose if I had lost the war, I would have been tried as a war criminal. Fortunately, we were on the winning side."[16]

~~~

Reading of what men did to other men and women and children in World War II makes me long to either weep or rail against a world I do not understand. Moreover, I am forced to ask that terrible question: what do these acts say about a fundamental quality of human nature? They say that killing comes easily to humans, once permission is given, far more easily than our moralists would like us to believe. James Jones in *The Thin Red Line* refers to the animal quality of American men in combat with Japanese soldiers.[17] Eugene Sledge in *With the Old Breed* repeats that story.[18] This quality of the animal is the essential link among all nations warring from 1939 to 1945: how quickly "ordinary men" sank into animals.

There exists in the human being some awful quality of cruelty and sadistic behavior that World War II brought forth in citizens of all warring nations. It is this quality of that war when linked to the quantity of those killed that distinguishes that war from all others, before or after. Horror characterizes that war, horror that rejects all thoughts of a "Good" war. The ability to kill so easily is not merely a quality of the German, Japanese, and Soviet soldier, it is English and American as well. For too long we have held ourselves aloof from the Holocaust, believing such destruction common to other nations, not to America.

The books of Victor Hanson, Max Boot, Steven Ambrose, and Tom Brokaw, the column of Scott Simon and the reporting on World War II and our other wars, have given America the certainty that it and its soldiers are not like those of other nations who rape and kill innocents. American soldiers are always heroic bands of brothers. But these myths and images of war help us deny the truth about ourselves, our animal-like nature in war. The United States can never come to terms with itself, its current actions, until it begins to understand that nature. Reports and books such as Ambrose's and Brokaw's particularly lead to lies about World War II, lies that, in the long run, deeply injure the country I so love. They allow us to believe that we were above the nastiness of the rest of the world, somehow purer than other nations. As long as we are so arrogant to believe that, we will become even more isolated in the world, unable to exercise real leadership.

~~~

That commonality in the ease of killing innocents on the part of all participants in World War II not only shows us their animal-like behavior, it also highlights their common achievements in science, technology, and bureaucracy and their ability to apply these skills to the demands of war.

Implied here is a conclusion I did not even want to consciously admit to myself for decades and almost refuse to examine: the scientific/technological/bureaucratic systems that evolved in both the United States and Germany in World War II had similar characteristics. At this level both countries conducted World War II in the same way. The similarities between mass killings in the concentration camp and mass killings from the air have scarcely ever been noted, but both actions require scientific theory, superior technologies, and efficient bureaucracies. As Paul Boyer wrote in *By the Bomb's Early Light*, "Perhaps after the passage of four decades, we are ready for a more comprehensive understanding of the moral disintegration wrought by World War II—an understanding that will at least consider in the same context (without necessarily equating) the atomic bomb and the gas chamber."[19] What might that context be? The first common context of the two techniques for killing innocents is the ability of those who invented and produced large-scale weapons of death in World War II to keep their own distance from that use. They worked in factories or laboratories, often far from the place where the killing was to occur. Clean places of work, decent food, leisure-time opportunities, a normal life, all these made it eminently possible to see their job as, quite simply, discovering a solution to a problem, whether that problem was the development and production of enough gas to kill a specified number of humans or the development and production of a new kind of bomb from a hitherto untapped source of power, atomic energy, able to kill an even greater number of humans. This distance from the place of killing was particularly true of the scientists in the United States, never threatened by bombing, never close to the consequences of the weapons they invented and prepared. The problem of new and more powerful weapons demanded technical solutions; the way the product was to be used probably seemed unimportant to some, even worse, unimaginable to others.

The second context, administration, by its very nature made the killing far easier. Paperwork never reeks with blood and saliva, sweat, urine, and feces released in fear and pain. The problem must be solved; much of the solution is made on paper. Supplies are requisitioned, tools ordered, equipment repaired, trains and trucks arranged to transport supplies and tools, production lines formed, products shipped from one plant to another and reconstituted into other products, shipped again to make the final product: a gas, a bomb, a weapon. Each task responds to paper, impersonal orders, demands, and requisitions that soon assume a godlike quality, never to be questioned. The paper must be obeyed.

The third context: far fewer men use the final product than produce it. The soldier at the end of the line who shoots a Jew in the back of the neck with his pistol is only one man; a great many more men and women are involved in the production of that pistol. And the same is true of the sword that sliced off the head of the terrified Chinese boy, kneeling before his Japanese captor. Finally, over time, fewer and fewer men are needed to perform the killing, the acts of barbarity at the end of the line where innocents are killed. Instead of one hundred men firing one hundred pistols to kill one hundred innocents, one man puts his foot on the gasoline pedal of his truck and pours carbon monoxide into the locked and windowless space behind him, killing the hundred, then one man dumps Zyklon B down a hole in a roof and kills two thousand. The culmination of mass killing occurs with a crew of ten or twelve flying an airplane over a city and killing one hundred thousand. With the bombs available today that same crew could, perhaps, kill one million.

Whether German, Japanese, English, American, or Soviet soldiers, when science, technology, and production combine, killing innocents with weapons that are increasingly more murderous becomes easier and easier. The ability to kill innocents at a distance, whether locked in a barren room into which Zyklon B drifts or prostrate beneath the searing force of napalm or the blinding sun of an atomic bomb, has become an essential characteristic of modern civilization.

Both means of killing are our inheritance from World War II.

~~~

The most frightening quality of this reality of modern, industrial war is that we as Americans have never really been aware of the terrible damage done in our name. We continue our daily and normal activities while our planes and weapons wreak havoc on innocent civilians. We never really understand or speak of the moral meaning and consequences of these actions, except in vague generalities such as "collateral damage."

No one has condemned the killing of innocents more poignantly than Fyodor Dostoyevsky did in 1880 in his introduction to the fable "The Grand Inquisitor," told by Ivan Karamazov to his brother, Alyosha, in *The Brothers Karamazov*:

> It was in the darkest days of serfdom, at the beginning of the nineteenth century. . . . There was in those days a general of aristocratic connections, the owner of great estates, one of those men . . . who, retiring from service into a life of leisure, are convinced that they've earned absolute power over the lives of their subjects. . . . So our general, settled on his property of two thousand souls . . . domineers over his poor neighbors as though they were dependents and buffoons. He has kennels of hundreds of hounds and nearly a hundred dog-boys—all mounted, and in uniform. One day a serf-boy, a little child of eight, threw a stone in play and hurt the paw of the general's favorite hound. "Why is my favorite dog lame?" He is told that the boy threw a stone that hurt the dog's paw. "So you did it." The general looked the child up and down. "Take him." He was taken—taken from his mother and kept shut up all night. Early that morning the general comes out on horseback, with the hounds, . . . his dog-boys, and huntsmen, all mounted around him in full hunting parade. . . . In front of them all stands the mother of the child. The child is brought from the lock-up. It's a gloomy, cold, foggy autumn day, a capital day

for hunting. The general orders the child to
be undressed; the child is stripped naked. He
shivers, numb with terror, not daring to cry.
. . . "Make him run," commands the general.
"Run! Run!" shout the dog-boys. The boy
runs. . . . "At him!" yells the general, and he
sets the whole pack of hounds on the child.
The hounds catch him, and tear him to pieces
before his mother's eyes![20]

Is it far-fetched to consider the killing of any
innocent child, either at a distance by bombs or
Zyklon B or up close by a bullet or a suicide bomber,
in the same category as this murder? Whether children are killed by dogs or bombs or bullets or fists
or swords, whether terrorists kill children, whether
the Israelis kill children, whether Americans kill children, it makes no difference. It is wrong, terribly,
terribly wrong for anyone to kill a child. It is, to use
an antiquated word, a "sin."

Now children are killed in war by the thousands
by bombing from a distance—our inheritance from
World War II and one of the qualities that make that
war so different from wars before. This warfare, often initiated by the push of a button three miles away,
is an accepted part of today's callousness. It has in-
troduced the world to a new way of death. American society has quite simply become so accustomed
to the killing of innocent children since the end of
World War II, that most of our media and our political leaders either refuse or are unable to express
moral outrage over facts so horrendous.

Since the tragic deaths of 9/11, as we seek revenge and demand justice, we have lost but few
soldiers compared to the number of enemy soldiers
and innocent civilians killed and wounded. Beyond
that, there has been no damage to Americans at

home while the destruction poured on our enemies has been unforgiving. Whole towns have been destroyed, women and children have been killed, earth shattered. We have reached swift military victories, collapsing now into guerrilla warfare where our soldiers have paid, are paying, and will pay enormous moral and physical costs for our occupation of Afghanistan and Iraq. In contrast, except for those innocents lost in the first attack on us on 9/11, Americans within our continental boundaries have paid little or no price for our invasions so far (unless, tragically, one of the troops killed or seriously wounded is a loved one). We are told by our president that our job is to go back to business as usual while we bomb other nations, far smaller than America, unable to defend themselves, unable to retaliate, many of those we injure and kill scarcely responsible for the horror of 9/11.

How have we come to accept the killing of innocents so easily, now a quality of our character and our power?

~~~

Once, even the morality of killing troops in battle was questioned.

In the 1920s, Ernest Hemingway wrote of World War I in *A Farewell to Arms*: "I was always embarrassed by the words sacred, glorious, and sacrifice and the expression in vain. We had heard them, sometimes standing in the rain almost out of earshot, so that only the shouted words came through, and had read them, on proclamations that were slapped up by billposters over other proclamations, now for a long time, and I had seen nothing sacred, and the things that were glorious had no glory and the sacrifices were like the stockyards of Chicago if nothing was done with the meat except to bury it. There were many words that you could not stand to hear and finally only the names of places had dignity."[21]

In the 1930s the great anti-war movie with Lew Ayres, *All Quiet on the Western Front*, was made and in that same decade Dalton Trumbo wrote his fine novel, *Johnny Got His Gun*, about a wounded war veteran, unable to speak or move but who still lived. In the 1960s other anti-war movies such as *Dr. Strangelove* appeared; in the 1980s *Platoon* and *Full Metal Jacket* showed the war in Vietnam realistically, even brutally. Yet, since then, little serious questioning of killing and wounding in war has occurred in the United States. Movies have turned World War II and our other wars into that glory and heroism Hemingway so decried while TV spectaculars do the same. Both now dominate our understanding of war.

Since World War II, the killing of innocents in war has become an accepted part of modern civilization, casually mentioned on TV, often referred to by that scurrilous euphemism, "collateral damage." Where have we gone wrong? Once we define a nation or a group of people as "Evil" there appears to be no limit to the damage we can inflict. As an embodiment of all the forces of evil, super-human, satanic, the enemy must be destroyed, its cities and infrastructure smashed, as Victor Davis Hanson suggests.[22]

The problems with such attitudes are several-fold. First, no matter how hard we try, our bombings do not discriminate. We cannot brand a piece of shrapnel as meant for combatant soldiers and order it to please stay away from civilians, particularly women and children. When we go to war in smaller countries and bomb safely from our fortress, we will kill civilians, make no mistake of this. Here,

Dostoyevsky raises a fundamental moral problem. As Ivan challenges his brother later in his preamble to his fable: if it were necessary to torture an innocent, "*one* tiny creature," (emphasis. mine) to make men happy, would it be right? To kill an innocent child, Ivan implies, no matter the purpose, destroys the moral order of the universe.[23]

Second, we are all, every citizen of the United States, morally complicit in the killing of innocents. We pay for the bombers, the bombs. Our elected representatives have given the executive branch of our government the right to kill as it sees fit. Each innocent killed rests on our conscience. There is no moral escape from our responsibility. To inflict pain without even understanding that pain is inflicted is one of the greatest of all moral failures. We become hard without knowing we are hard, separated from the suffering we ourselves have caused. We no longer care that death and pain are inflicted in our name. We no longer grasp how much we are hated in the world for our carelessness and insensitivity.

Third, this chasm between the nature of our power, its terrible force, and our morality, began with the weapons we used in World War II. Over sixty years of war they have swiftly evolved, allowing us to kill innocent civilians in greater numbers at a greater distance, while we, the citizens of America, are free to go about our daily business, protected by oceans and our armed forces. Our indifference forms a hard shell over our humanity. We no longer understand that our power is based on another's pain. We no longer understand that each time we kill or wound an innocent we make twenty more enemies, his or her family, tribe, and clan, all potential terrorists. This killing of innocents not only has disastrous impacts upon us morally, it is also a stupid thing to do strategically and tactically. It may lead to victory, but it often leaves a lingering quality of disgust that coats any claim of triumph. It is also certain to breed revenge in this era of the suicide bomber. Our troops are the ones who pay the moral and the physical price for our insensitivity: killing in retaliation becomes their function and their task.

Is this then an America of which we can be proud? We won a great victory in World War II. Is its consequence to be only the formation of another empire, built on deadly weapons with the threat of killing innocents the basis for our power?

CHAPTER 2

The Moral Dilemma of the Combat Infantryman

While I read about "killing" in our media descriptions of the war in Iraq, my thoughts resonated with my memory of World War II and my short time in combat before I was wounded. I never killed anyone—or so I believe as I only fired one shot in the fog of battle—yet I saw men killed, even stepped on a dead German soldier in the middle of a night firefight, and was terrified of being killed myself. It is that personal experience with killing and fear of being killed that has so separated me from most of my fellow Americans who have no understanding of the meaning of war beyond the clichés—lies, I would say—of the media. They simply either do not grasp or refuse to consider what the combat infantrymen they send overseas actually do: either kill or wound other human beings while terrified of death or wounding themselves.

Killing is the goal of the combat infantryman. Killing is also his—hers now, too—moral dilemma. Yet the men or women who, in service to their country, perform the act of killing and fear the act of being killed, are often the most isolated human beings in America when they return home: they speak a language that cannot be understood in their native land. They endure a loneliness unknown to most of their countrymen and women. They simply learn not to speak of their feelings, finally repressing all memories of what they once did and what was done to them, or else they nourish those memories through acts of self-destruction from alcohol to drugs to rape to robbery to murder to suicide, often enduring homelessness.

Much of my life since experiencing battle has centered on understanding this moral dilemma of killing in combat for the American soldier, the only time men and women—except as members of a police force, national, state, or local—are given societal permission to kill another human being. How willing are our soldiers to kill? How does the act of killing impact them? What happens to them after the killing ends? Does the willingness to kill change over time?

The most frustrating (even infuriating) aspect of my search for answers to these questions is how little is written about them, how uncomfortable they make most people, how there are such conflicting opinions about what it means for the infantryman to kill. We treat our soldiers in war as heroes, welcome them with loving arms. We read of their exploits, see their acts on television. Yet, when it comes to the brutal reality of the world of combat they experience, a place without pity, we always draw a curtain. We refuse to show the dead on TV as they really appear. We refuse to deal with the reality of our soldiers killing others, sometimes innocents, women and children. We refuse to admit that "missing in action" usually implies that the soldier's body has disappeared, blown into small parts by artillery fire. We refuse to acknowledge what the soldier at war has actually done: taken other lives with our approval.

And, so, the soldier who comes home from combat has no one to whom he can really talk. He shuts up, never pours out his true feelings, what he has really seen, the acts committed. Of all the disservices we do to our troops, our treatment of them on returning home is by far the worst. It is time, I think, to deal with what the word "killing" really means in combat, what it has meant over generations, and how that meaning has changed in this century of killing beginning in 1914 with World War I.

~~~

J. Glenn Gray in his book *The Warriors* expresses one opinion about killing in World War II:

> Anyone who has watched men on the battlefield at work with artillery, or looked into the eyes of veteran killers fresh from slaughter, or studied the description of bombardiers' feelings while smashing their targets, finds hard to escape the conclusion that there is a delight in destruction. . . . Men who have lived in the zone of combat long enough to be veterans are sometimes possessed by a fury that makes them capable of anything. Blinded by the rage to destroy and supremely careless of consequences, they storm against the enemy until they are either victorious, dead, or utterly exhausted. It is as if they are seized by a demon.[1]

And Bill Mauldin in *Up Front* says exactly the opposite:

> But you don't become a killer. No normal man who has smelled and associated with

death ever wants to see any more of it. In fact, the only men who are even going to want to bloody noses in a fist fight after this war will be those who want people to think they were tough combat men, when they weren't. The surest way to become a pacifist is to join the infantry.[2]

Not only are opinions about killing in the infantry in World War II in conflict, I have discovered in years of reading about war and battle that most serious and almost all popular literature assiduously avoids the real meaning of killing in combat. I have only managed to discover some answers to this unstated and deeply repressed moral and emotional problem of combat killing by examining another controversy about the American soldier in battle: what proportion of American soldiers at the front actually fired their weapons when in a firefight in World War II? One of the most interesting phenomena following World War II was the rage engendered by the findings of Brig. Gen. S. L. A. (SLAM) Marshall about the combat infantryman in that war. Based on interviews he conducted with U.S. soldiers after their combat experience, he concluded that around seventy-five to eighty-five percent probably did not fire their weapons when at the front line in both the Pacific and European Theater of Operations.[3]

In the *American Heritage* magazine of March 1989, Fredric Smoler wrote an article attacking Marshall's findings.[4] He leaned heavily on the work of Capt. Harold Leinbaugh of the 84th Infantry Division, in combat in Europe from November 1944 to May of 1945. Leinbaugh wrote and published *The Men of Company K* along with John Campbell, a memoir of the combat experience of his company in the 84th.[5] Over time, Marshall's findings had angered Leinbaugh.

He, in turn, contacted the military historian, Roger Spiller, founder and deputy head of the Combat Studies Institute at Fort Leavenworth, Kansas.

Together, Leinbaugh and Spiller questioned Marshall's methods, even his integrity. They discredited Marshall's interviews, research techniques, and conclusions as well as Marshall's claims about his service record in World War I. In *The Deadly Brotherhood* by John C. McManus, published in 1998, the attack on Marshall's findings continued. McManus flatly states that, "Marshall's claim was and is absurd and is based on no factual evidence of any kind."[6]

Such sharply conflicting and angry opinions over the conclusions of one military historian about the combat actions of World War II infantrymen, conclusions developed almost sixty years ago, tell me that something else is occurring, of far greater significance than simply the number of soldiers who fired or did not fire in combat in World War II.

The issue among all these conflicting opinions is not about the proportion of American men who fired in combat but of the willingness of American men to kill enemy soldiers. Perhaps the ending of Smoler's article in *American Heritage* gives one side of the equation best: "Leinbaugh and Spiller—and the evidence—suggest the truth is more prosaic: In battle's hard school, ordinary people [American soldiers] eventually discover, quite by themselves, the knack of skillful killing."[7]

In contrast, Marshall states that, "it is therefore reasonable to believe that the average and normally healthy individual—the man who can endure the mental and physical stresses of combat—still has such an inner and usually unrealized resistance toward killing a fellow man that he will not of his own volition take life if it is possible to turn away from that responsibility. . . . At the vital point he becomes a conscientious objector, unknowing." Marshall further wrote, "I well recall that in World War I the great sense of relief that came to troops [after they left the line] was due . . . to the blessed knowledge that for a time they were not under the compulsion to take life."[8]

This is a startling statement: that men in World War I did not want to take life, were not the killers of our clichés. It is an insight seldom explored or discussed in the literature of combat yet one with important consequences for our understanding of battle. We deal here with two fundamentally different interpretations of the American soldier in war: on the one side, men are easily capable of learning to kill with impunity; on the other side, they are far more humane, repelled by the act of killing. The conflict over Marshall's findings is about the soldier's willingness to kill, not over his ability to shoot.

For me, any adequate discussion of this conflict over the willingness of the American soldier to kill in combat requires a brief review of the history of attitudes toward killing in war, its slow evolution over time.

Over centuries in the Roman Catholic Church, rooted in the commandment "thou shall not kill," the just war theory slowly evolved, formed, first, by Catholic thinkers of the Medieval Ages from Augustine to Aquinas. "As restated in 1983 by the United States Catholic bishops, a 'just war' must meet several criteria: be absolutely necessary, waged by a competent authority, use comparative justice (that is, only such force as is necessary), fought with the right intentions, begun only after peaceful means of settlement have been exhausted, have some probability of success, and the costs incurred be proportionate to the expected good."[9] Within this frame killing in war is allowed. Further conventions control how that killing is to be done.

In the early days of the Christian church even those rules were sometimes accepted with great reluctance. As noted by Thomas Merton in his slim book *Ways of the Christian Mystics,* "In the ninth and tenth centuries, even killing in war was regarded as a sin requiring expiation. In the Anglo-Saxon penitential of Theodore of Canterbury, a soldier who killed a man in war was obliged to a forty-day fast even though he might have killed his enemy in the 'ordinary line of duty,' under obedience to his officer. Later penitentials distinguished between offensive and defensive killing. One who attacked an enemy and killed him was obliged to do penance. One who killed another in self-defense was not obliged to do penance but was *counseled* to do so for the good of his soul. Burchard of Worms, in the eleventh century, equated killing in war with ordinary homicide and assigned *seven* years of penance, without distinction as to offense or defense" (emphasis mine).[10]

English common law also dealt with the problem of killing. It posed the concept "a duty to retreat" at the core of conditions that might lead to legitimate killing. A person when attacked had the responsibility to use every reasonable means to retreat before resorting to violence.[11] Wars in the eighteenth century were organized about this principle. As Page Smith indicates in *A New Age Now Begins,* "The fighting was done by small professional armies that were expensive to train and maintain and were thus, for the most part, used sparingly . . . [in wars in which] the enemy, being outmaneuvered and surrounded, might be persuaded to surrender after having fought boldly enough to preserve his honor and without extensive loss of life on either side."[12]

In the United States during the Civil War and our Indian wars that concept was radically restructured to another approach to warfare, rooted only in killing: unconditional surrender. The "enemy"—whoever, whenever, wherever—was to be given no escape, destroyed, pummeled, beaten into dust. The ruthless destruction of Sherman's march through the South and the murderous crushing of the Indian tribes in our battles against them point to the acceptance, no, the near delight, of destroying the enemy in "unconditional surrender," qualities of American character totally inimical to Christian morality opposed to killing in war.[13] In state and federal supreme courts the "duty to retreat" rule of English common law was replaced after the Civil War with the "true man" concept of the frontier: a threatened man had the right to defend himself.[14]

Even in World War I however, that earlier morality, as Marshall so carefully observed, still survived in the American combat soldier: a reluctance to kill. The conclusion that Marshall reaches about American soldiers killing in combat in World War I was rooted in this far earlier Christian morality—"thou shall not kill." He believed that faith in this biblical commandment against killing simply controlled men's actions then more strongly than in recent wars. Killing once was, quite simply, a repulsive act, one not to be undertaken by a decent man. Even when state and federal law allowed killing in self-defense, even when that rule was expanded in combat to include killing in war, the act of killing still troubled the ordinary man.

At issue between Marshall and his critics is how much the ordinary soldier felt repugnance over killing in World War II. Much happened to change the morality of America in those years between the end of World War I in 1918 and the beginning of World

War II in America in 1941. By that year, when the attack on Pearl Harbor occurred and America declared war on Japan, Germany, and Italy, the moral control over killing in combat must have begun its slow decline. The peace movement that had so marked the early and middle 1930s had slowly evaporated as the horror of Hitler's Nazi Germany became clear to many Americans. The Great Depression had driven the world into a moral despair and great fear. At the same time in the 1930s the world quickly went mad with killing and the rage of war: Japan invaded China; Italy ravaged Abyssinia (Ethiopia today) and began the bombing of civilians; the Spanish Civil War erupted and bombing escalated in the destruction of Guernica; the rape of Nanking occurred; Germany invaded Poland, defeated France, bombed England, then invaded Russia. Stories of war, photographs of war, newsreels of war, these were the daily fare of young American men; war as glory, war as heroism were their certain destiny. In 1940 the first peacetime draft took them into the army. In 1941 Pearl Harbor took them into war and the long attrition of World War II. America's dedication to "Remember Pearl Harbor" formed their fate. The "duty to kill" became our mantra.

It took defeats in such battles as Kasserine Pass in North Africa to finally harden our combat troops to the act of killing. The British partially blamed those defeats on American's lack of a will to fight.[15] Only after further "hard" fighting did the soldier become the "killer" his leaders desired.

World War II became a moment of transition from one morality over killing to another. The policy toward killing in World War II was clear: as stated by Capt. Reuben E. Jenkins in a review of FM (Field Manual) 100-5, "Blood is the price of victory. One must accept the formula or not wage war."[16]

It is my guess that Marshall used the lens of his experience in World War I, when men were more reluctant to kill, to view the relation between killing and the combat infantryman of World War II, while his critics of today see the combat infantryman of World War II from their perspective of the wars fought since 1945. Killing, even in combat, was still viewed as abhorrent in 1917–1918. By 1941–1945 the moral restraints on killing in war had begun to loosen.

Evidence accumulated since the end of World War II indicates that moral restraint on the act of killing in war by the American soldier has shifted even more than it did between World War I and World War II. Perhaps beginning in Korea, but certainly in Vietnam and in our wars of empire since then, the American soldier appears to be at far greater ease with the act of killing. The body count in Vietnam, the massacre of civilians at My Lai (and other places in Vietnam most certainly); the horrendous ratio of casualties we inflicted in Somalia—five hundred Somalis killed, eighteen Americans; the ratio of killing in Iraq in the Gulf War—approximately one hundred thousand Iraqi soldiers to one hundred forty-eight Americans; the continuing slaughter of Taliban and al Qaeda fighters in Afghanistan with far fewer American casualties than Afghans; the fact that we kill and wound far more Iraqi insurgents than they kill and wound us, all point to what I believe to be a change in the combat soldier's moral attitude about killing. In fact, a Marine sergeant in Vietnam once said, "One of the most brutal things in the world is your average nineteen-year-old American boy."[17]

Thus, both Marshall and his critics appear to be right: Marshall spoke of the soldier in an earlier America, a time of far greater simplicity and morality. His critics speak of the America we have become, a far different place where violence and its partner, killing, are simply a part of life, from the school shootings at Columbine to the vulgarity of our media reports of murder and rapine. World War II was a time of transition from one morality for controlling killing in war to another. It marks that moment in American history when the force of a moral opposition to killing waned.

~~~

Though it is difficult, probably impossible, to even estimate the cause of such monumental changes in attitudes toward killing in war, some tentative ideas can be presented.

Along with the rise since 1945 in such anti-social realities as murder, rape, and sexual abuse has come a breakdown in both the American community and the American family. As Robert Putnam points out in his book, *Bowling Alone*, the "social capital" of the American community has declined.[18] Simply put, people devote less time to volunteer efforts of all kinds that lie at the roots of any community: elections, school boards, city council meetings, church attendance, etc.—all such activities receive less support. Lack of time, lack of interest, a whole variety of reasons suffice as causes.

At the same time divorce rates, though falling, still remain high.[19] Illegitimate births range near 70 percent for some groups.[20] The father is often absent. Mothers must work with inadequate child care. In marriages that do survive, both partners often have to work to make an adequate living. The consequence? Latchkey kids, kids without supervision, the TV left as their parental guide; babies never receiving the caring required to become responsible adults. Aggression patrols our streets in automobile drivers who test each other; our use of vulgar epithets and bad manners emphasizes the disintegration of human relations; competition in business has increased to an almost vicious quality; the media worships violence and killing. Violence of the grossest kind dominates TV. Video games about World War II, such as *Call of Duty*, instruct the players on how to kill German soldiers.[21] Innumerable others are built around the "thrill" of killing.

In all these instances a blatant individualism is expressed: the ego reigns supreme. The child who grows up to become the combat soldier of today has often received little training in moral repugnance over acts of aggression and killing in the civilian world. In a real way TV and the movies glorify killing. Why should he or she worry about its morality in the military where the soldier's purpose is discovered in killing? Permission to kill comes with the uniform. The restraint once imposed on the soldier in the killing zone no longer has the social, communal, and familial force it once had as part of the common man's moral fiber.

Connected to these incredible changes in the ease with which killing becomes acceptable to America and, then, to the American combat soldier, is the way the soldier's weaponry has increased in killing capacity. In my war, World War II, the infantryman's weapon was the M-1 Garand rifle, which fired only eight rounds to the clip. Now the M-16 clip has twenty rounds that can be fired on full automatic. All other weapons used by the individual soldier have increased their lethal quality in a similar evolution. Now, helicopter gun ships hover above the ground spraying hundreds of rounds of murderous ammunition on enemy troops who cannot hide below. Night-vision goggles let the killing continue in the dark. Killing has, quite simply, become much easier for the American soldier in combat.

Thus, those writers who insist that the American soldier easily learns to kill are identifying certain qualities of modern American life: the breakdown of social controls over violence and killing in our society coupled with our development of more murderous weaponry. Marshall's world of combat existed in a simpler era, in terms of community, family, and military technology, times when killing was seen far differently than today. Then, killing was wrong and killing in combat was a moral choice the soldier could make.

Today, and even toward the end of World War II, killing by the combat soldier seems to have become an accepted, even highly approved of quality of modern life. The battle evidence in Somalia, the Gulf War, Afghanistan, and now Iraq certainly supports this conclusion. The idea of penance for the act of killing is no longer even considered after a "kill" is reported by the American soldier.

In fact, if suggested, it would be ridiculed. Rather, praise for a kill is the soldier's reward. The concept of guilt for killing in war seems no longer to exist to the extent it did as recently as in World War I, as once it did a thousand years ago in times now considered primitive, "medieval," being a common expression for a backward, cruel, rapacious people. One must actually ask: which era had the greater regard for human morality around the issue of killing? Ours or medieval times?

～〜～

And yet, in spite of these monumental changes in social values and the technology of killing, one still hears the wistful echo of moral repugnance over the act of killing in combat: the stigma, the shame following the killing of another human being still haunts the combat soldier. A most poignant article in the *New York Times* at the beginning of the war in Iraq emphasized that this terrible moral dilemma for the combat infantryman still exists. Sergeant Mark N. Redmond said after only a few days of combat, "I mean, I have my wife and kids to go back home to. I don't want them to think I'm a killer. . . . When I go home, people will treat me like I'm a hero, but I'm not. I'm a Christian man. If I have to kill the other guy I will, but it doesn't make me a hero. I just want to go home to my wife and kids." And the chaplain for the Brigade of the Third Division said, "We're in the thousands now that were killed in the last few days. Nothing prepares you to kill another human being. Nothing prepares you to use a machine gun to cut someone in two. . . . It bothers them to take life, especially that close."[22]

In other reports conscientious objectors to the war in Iraq, already in the army, sometimes are given CO status and honorably discharged. In other cases they are court martialed, stripped of rank and privileges, jailed, given a dishonorable discharge. One combat soldier, home from Iraq, said, "It becomes a very religious thing, because I wonder, you know, since I've taken these lives, if I'm going to be accepted into heaven. You know, have I done the right thing?"[23]. In spite of all the changes in social values and the evolutions in killing machines, that repugnance at taking another life still resonates within some ordinary human beings. The fact that society gives the combat soldier the right to kill is the quality that makes war so different from all other human endeavors. The fact that society also gives that soldier new technology that makes killing far easier than ever in history makes the modern American warrior far more likely to experience killing and its agonizing stresses than in earlier wars.

Is it time, perhaps, to recognize this enormous moral and emotional burden we place on the combat infantryman? Time to realize that this burden is carried for the rest of the soldier's life, hidden in a society that neither admits nor understands what the grunt at the front does, his acts certain to eat at him in ways no civilian can ever grasp? As James Russell Lowell wrote during the Mexican-American War of 1846–1848 in *The Biglow Papers:*

Ef you take a sword an' dror it,
An' go stick a feller thru,
Guv'ment aint to answer for it,
God'll send the bill to you.[24]

The individual combat soldier, not the nation-state, is the one who pays for a lifetime the emotional price for his acts in war. We should, therefore, be careful about sending our young men and women into harm's way, recognizing that it is not only the danger of killing and wounding that the combat soldier faces, it is also the impact on his life-long emotional, spiritual, and moral integrity that is at risk.

~~~

The myth of the "Good War" makes no allowance for such subtleties. The soldiers who fought in World War II were all heroes. They never had any moral problems with killing; killing was the accepted act to perform. The enemy was evil and had to be eradicated. Our heroes performed that act . . . and never soiled themselves in the process, never suffered a lifetime of silence over their wartime killings. We believe, out of the Myths of World War II, that the soldier can kill without paying any spiritual or moral price and that his nation also pays no such price for his act. Is this the world we really want to support?

CHAPTER 3

The Impact of World War II on Its Soldiers

One of the costs of killing and wounding in war we seldom consider, except, briefly, in the midst of a war, is what the killing does to soldiers and civilians after the war is over, often resulting in Post Traumatic Stress Disorder (PTSD). With America's wars in Korea and Vietnam, with its decision to use violence as the way to stop terrorism, with our consequent wars in Third World nations, with the atrocious war our soldiers now fight in Iraq and its disastrous impact on our soldiers and Iraqi civilians there, it is simply time to recognize that the United States lives in a world shadowed by experiences of war and that those experiences totally change the way some of our citizens perceive reality. We have created a special class of people, the wounded of war in body and spirit, a class apart, a class we never see, outside the mainstream, often unable to hold a job, homeless, drunk, criminal, addicted to drugs, and sometimes suicidal.

I speak of this from a lifetime of over sixty years living with the impact of PTSD. From September 1944 when I was badly wounded in the liberation of France from the Nazis to the winter of 2004–2005, when I experienced my latest episode of PTSD, my life has

been crippled by the emotional and physical consequences of that wound. I have learned that one never
"gets over" Post Traumatic Stress Disorder. Though
one is able to manage it so that it no longer destroys
life, it is always there, buried in the psyche, ready to
attack when the right trigger is squeezed.

Each time we read of those experiencing a terrorist attack, pursued by guerrilla forces, or
wounded, even participating, in a firefight, we really are being told of people whose lives will never
be the same again. Their fundamental trust in the
nature of reality is smashed for many years, a trust
extremely difficult to rebuild. My years after adoles-
cence have been shadowed by that moment when I
was blown up by German artillery fire east of Verdun.
My right buttock and lower back were sheared off, a
piece of shrapnel shattered my skull and penetrated
the left parietal area of my brain, paralyzing my right
side, and another piece of shrapnel halted its path
in my pelvic area. When I read of those men and
women following 9/11 who are still incapable of
leaving their apartments over four years later I understand their PTSD and so wish I could reach out
and hold them in my arms and let them weep themselves into exhaustion. When I read of our troops in
Iraq, I wither inside as I imagine their future: to have
been in mortal danger in a place so alien in land-
scape and in culture, then, suddenly, to be trans-
ported back to this fat and greedy nation with its
expressways and SUVs, its six thousand square foot
houses, its TV that turns battle into a morbid joke,
its supermarkets with their glut of goods, its media's
dedication to violence, its people who have sacri-
ficed nothing in this war, except for those few families who have lost their loved ones, its people who
have no understanding of what war is really like,
while its troops grope for life in a half-mad environ-

ment where the enemy is unknown and one kills civilians by mistake. This is enough to drive one beyond reason to insanity.

I understand deeply their fear and rage. In a nation that so strongly believes in control over one's life, in the ability to reach success on one's own terms, the nature of such emotional pain forever separates the discharged combat soldier from his peers.

Siegfried Sassoon, the great World War I English poet, wrote of that war:

War was a fiend who stopped our clocks
Although we met him grim and gay.[1]

This is an exact description of what happens to those of us traumatically injured in war or terrorism by willful acts of another human being. Our clocks are stopped at one moment in time. The rest of our lives are devoted to restarting those clocks. For some the time is never changed. As Sergeant Louis Simpson, poet and Pulitzer Prize winner and former combat soldier of World War II, said, "My bet would be that anyone who's seen real combat would have for the rest of his life something going on inside him. Some wound. Some secret."[2]

For me, at least, and I think for many others, this after-combat experience is not only one of depression. As I have thought over a lifetime: would to God PTSD were as simple as depression. PTSD is steeped in alienation, the deepest sense of rejection and betrayal by the world, so much so that it is physical in nature, just as my wound was physical, the rending of my flesh, unable to talk, move, speak, great quantities of blood gushing over my hands, thick and red, and sweetly smelling. Like all those who experience PTSD, in an instant's explosion I became a stranger to myself. At one moment I was a badly frightened boy of nineteen who had just crossed the Canal des Mines west of the Moselle River under fire, the next I was someone I did not know. The certainty that there is a stranger within me has haunted all my days and many of my nights. The terrible sense of alienation and isolation that comes to me when this uninvited stranger arrives paralyzes me, fills the world with darkness, turns those I love into strangers. When some experience, usually unexpected and unannounced, usually involving external authority, triggers my unconscious memory of wounding and betrayal, I can, in a moment of time so short it cannot be measured, descend into an inward doom, asking that most terrible of questions: who is this stranger that suddenly dominates my being? Who am I? Worst of all: whom can I trust?

When I was young and had no real idea of what was happening to me, the isolation as I descended into this gray and grim inward room frightened me beyond the telling of it. For, then, there was no help for my condition, no one to talk to about the shattering of my psyche and my flesh by violence. The psychiatrist I went to after the war was a good man but he traced my despair to my mother, father, the Oedipus tragedy. Oh, that did play a part in my pain but the core of the problem rose from the simple fact that I had almost been killed, killed by a stranger who wanted my death. Not merely that my flesh had been rent but that the decimation had come from the will of another, one whom I would have killed.

For me, it has always been this aspect of my wound that made its healing so incredibly difficult: an anonymous stranger wanted my death and I had wanted his. It is this condition we are never really allowed to speak of when we come home, one that is never really understood: the combat soldier is simultaneously engaged in an attempt to kill another human being while experiencing the fear of being killed. The decent person—and most soldiers are decent people—often cannot live with the awful meaning of this dilemma. Recovering from that reality has taken me a lifetime.

Looking back at the process of healing, I can now see its steps with enormous clarity. They begin with anger, with an all-consuming, fiery anger that nothing could quench. I still have my journals from the spring of 1945 when I came home from the war, discharged, alone in our small town, all my friends overseas. I cry now when I read those entries, that young boy so hurt, so frightened, so enraged, absolutely alone:

> Here lies Ed Wood, wifeless, childless,
> Wishing his father had died the same.

That anger was like an insatiable fire burning within. Alcohol might help but it didn't really dull the rage. Smashing a fist against the wall and knocking a hole in the plaster only scarred my knuckles. Marrying. Divorcing. Sleeping around. Running to a foreign nation. Nothing salved the pain. The fundamental trust in other human beings had been broken. Everyone, everything becomes an enemy: strike back before one is hit again.

Trust no one.

~~~

Yet, if one is lucky, one neither hurts oneself or others, the fires slowly bank. Though they never die out, they burn low after years. Fourteen years passed after I was wounded before I began to have a career. Fourteen years of some schooling, terrible jobs, struggling to write, being rejected, living outside the United States, failing at marriage, fathering three children, working alone out-of-doors where I was not required to communicate with others. Then almost twenty years of a successful career, money, prestige, power. And yet—and this is the fact that both the nation and those who suffer PTSD need to face—the stranger within me never left, was always there, ready to shape and mold my behavior at the slightest opportunity. The emotion within was, most of all, a vast uncertainty, a confusion as to how to act, a retreat within, a fear of contact, an overwhelming fear of death, and a brooding disaster.

Now, in looking back on all those years I can see so clearly the pattern in which I lived, understand the emotional triggers that were always poised to free that stranger within so that I became, again, a stranger to myself, lost in an instant, overwhelmed with uncertainty and fear. Sometimes it was an authority figure that triggered my PTSD. It might begin with filling out a form for some bureaucracy. It might be a meeting gone sour. It might be a chance word by the drinking fountain in an office. It might be the income tax every year. It might be my boss. Sometimes it was an act of violence as when I was robbed at the point of a gun. Another time it occurred when thieves broke into my apartment and trashed it. My most recent incident was sparked by a traffic accident, my fault. No one was hurt, thank God, though our car was totaled. But, for me, a moment of the most intense trauma: recalling that instant when I was hit.

I have puzzled over my inward trauma for a lifetime. I understand why those acts of violence, from being robbed to the screech of metal on metal in an accident, echo with memories of shellfire, fear, crouching in a ditch, attaching a bayonet to my rifle, the blow of shrapnel, the eruption of that stranger within. But I have always struggled with why an external, impersonal authority or its symbol so terrifies me, brings back that haunting feeling of lying alone, paralyzed, blood gushing from my skull, unable to speak or talk. My old friend Bob Reed, also a former infantryman, who had his left hand blown off by mortar fire in the South Pacific, has exactly this same reaction to authority. We've tried to understand in conversations why we both have had similar triggers to our PTSD from the time we met in college in 1945 to as recently as yesterday. And we've both spent countless hours with psychiatrists searching for some equanimity.

Our conclusion? When we were wounded we lost control of "ourselves," who we really were, to an authority far greater than ourselves, an impersonal, all-powerful force, an "enemy" that smashed us into insensibility so that an alienated stranger within us came to control our being. All these minor authorities with whom we deal each day, from boss to auditor to policeman, have sometimes seemed to possess that same impersonal power as the German or Japanese soldier who fired the shell that rent us. That authority threatens us with the same loss of self: in that instant of impersonal, authoritarian threat, we become strangers to ourselves, exactly the same emotions as when we were wounded. Such "attacks," if that is the proper word, have become quite simply part of who we are. From the most minor of things—did I turn off the stove?—to the most major—did I put my check in the income tax return or in my payment for my ticket from my accident?—many days are spent in a vast uncertainty that some authority may seize us and many nights, for me at least, are lost in a constant nightmare: that an authority has condemned me to a coffin-size cell and I lie there, paralyzed, impotent, in darkness, a terror I defy others to experience.

Since we were blown up by shellfire the two of us have trusted almost nothing. And, of course, this is not true only of those of us wounded in World War II. Two friends of mine, in their fifties now, fought in Vietnam, one with two tours of duty. Both have been terribly injured by their experience as Bob and I were. Both have run as Bob and I did—both still search for their meaning, both still driven by that fierce energy of those hurt or wounded in combat.

Around four hundred thousand of our young men and women have been killed or wounded in military service since World War II. I wonder, now, how many of our soldiers, particularly those in Iraq and Afghanistan, will struggle over long years with what they did and what was done to them in Baghdad, Fallujah, Najaf, Kandahar, and will desperately seek to start their clocks again. Participation in combat, being wounded in combat, creates a group of Americans forever separate from the nation, their experience forever foreign to their peers. In the deepest sense, no matter how successful they become, they are always cripples, shadowed by a darkness not known to others.

~᠀~

And, yet—and this I know is the paradox—Bob and I have lived meaningful lives. Bob has traveled around the world, seen things that few of us ever dare to even imagine. He was arrested picketing for civil liberties shortly after the war, has explored the New Guinea jungle, knew headhunters there, bummed through Europe in the late 1940s when it remained a destroyed wasteland, graduated from the University of Chicago, participated in the Selma march in 1965, served on a team of seven who attempted to bring the Cook County jail out of the nineteenth century, helped halt capital punishment in Illinois, owned and ran an inn in Morocco, became one of the few Western men to ride a camel across the Sahara Desert with Tuaregs, and, finally, ran an important and successful drug rehabilitation program.[3]

My life has not been half so romantic; I graduated from a prestigious eastern university and, as a city planner, held high positions in cities and consulting firms across the nation. When that played out, partially because I no longer believed in it—the developer had taken central stage—but also because dealing with authority in so many ways was simply more emotionally exhausting than I could take, I went back to France and stood by the Canal de Mines where the artillery shell had shredded my flesh as a boy-soldier forty years earlier. It was if I were two persons for an instant, that young soldier and this older man. The sudden union of past and present began a slow healing within myself. I decided that what I must do was become my own authority on the nature of violence and war that had haunted me all my life. I quit city planning and began to read, then write, about violence and war as central aspects of the American national character. In twenty-five years I have published three books, several articles, poetry, and have finished a long semi-autobiographical novel and am working on another that deals with an unknown tragedy of World War II: the Army Specialized Training Program, which, after closing, threw thousands of young men without adequate training into the infantry, many into combat.[4] All these pieces of writing center on issues of war and peace, violence and compassion.

Both of the Vietnam combat vets I know have also followed different careers. They are now writers living outside the United States. All of us would say with absolute certainty that it is the fierce energy generated by our wounds and the Post Traumatic Stress Disorder that followed us that lies at the core of our accomplishments and our lives.

~∾~

The perspective through which Bob and I and so many veterans of combat view World War II, all wars for that matter, is thus extraordinarily different from that of the normal American. We see war from the pain of our PTSD. We see war from sixty years of struggling with the consequences of our wounds, sixty years of watching war after war after war dirty the nation and the globe, shocking other young men and women into their PTSD. We see it from the front line as former infantrymen, from the fear of the grunt under fire, from his rage as friends die like butchered animals, from the brutality our soldiers inflict on others out of their own anger, from the reality of their betrayal. We see the unintended consequences of war.

We know that World War II was not the "Good War" fought by the "Greatest Generation." We saw the war in Vietnam for its terrible tragedy. We see the war in Iraq that way, the half-mad environment of the combat infantrymen, young men and women who could be my grandchildren, to be haunted forever by their acts of battle as Bob and I have been. We know that combat soldiers are the only ones who see war for what it really is, understand what it will do to those young soldiers for their long lives. Sixty years from now they, too, will suffer from within, never to be the men or women they might have been.

We ask:

● Are there other directions for us to lead the nations of this earth, beyond the Myths of World War II, beyond this insistent demand for the eradication of enemies through our position as the world's super power?

● Are there ways of peace we can create that will keep our young men and women, the men and women—young, old, and, yes, their children—of the whole world from living the life of alienation Bob and I have experienced?

● Are there other ways to struggle with our newest enemies, terrorists, so as to avoid such pain?

~~~

As these three chapters have shown, there was no "Good War." World War II made the killing of innocents at a distance part of our national character. It burdened the combat soldier with an insufferable decision: the dilemma of killing. It often controlled the rest of his life with the impact of PTSD. But, once the killing in France and Germany, China and the Philippines began, it is certain that it was a w; America had to fight. It was a war that, toward end, showed no mercy to any participants, sol and civilian. Cruel beyond the telling of it, it h ened those who struggled at the front, corr those who administered it behind the line. I and wounding became normal. Suffering was massive, the common bond of many peoples of the world.

Yet, the United States, except for members of the armed forces, their friends and families, experienced a war so different from that of other nations it might have been fought on another planet. Instead of being bombed as in England and the Continent, it knew a greater prosperity than ever in its history. Instead of occupation and its companions, repression, imprisonment, torture, and slow starvation, as in France and Holland, Belgium and Poland, Hungary and Romania, Yugoslavia and Greece, incomes and savings spiraled in the United States. Instead of terrorized flights from warring armies, rapine and death, scorched earth and homelessness, career and job opportunities exploded. Instead of animal-like firefights in the South Pacific, great escapes on weekends were enjoyed, while, as always, the repression of minorities was ignored, the cruelties to the Japanese justified.

The agonies of the rest of the world were never experienced by most Americans, being neither bombed nor killed nor wounded, having to neither bomb nor kill nor wound, never suffering the agonies of PTSD. The nation so easily believed the stories of war promulgated by movies and books, and, later, television, written and produced by men and women who never faced that moral dilemma of killing another human being, who believed that war was a pleasurable duty the patriot must perform. The words that Hemingway so loathed as a younger writer, heroism and glory, slowly glossed the reality of what a few of us had known.

The war had given America a great prosperity. The real truth behind our prosperity could not be told.

So the war must have been "Good." And, if so, was not war in itself a "Good?" After all, war saved us from the threat of Hitler and the "bestial" Japanese. It made us the wealthiest nation in the world. It made for great movies. Its wartime industries took us out of the Great Depression. The myth of the "Good War" was born, and the killing of innocents, the moral dilemma of our combat infantryman, the reality of PTSD were repressed, seldom to reach the surface of our corporate mind.

Part II

The Second Myth:
"The Greatest Generation"

CHAPTER 4

On Judging Artistic Interpretations of World War II

Turning a generation that fought a major war into the "Greatest Generation" is common in American history. Those who fought and won the American Revolution were honored long after their war with similar accolades. By the 1890s the generation that fought the Civil War had replaced the pain and murderous battles with memories far softer, those of glory and honor and sacrifice. For all our wars, granite and marble monuments, decorated with the bravest of words, became the way to memorialize memories long dead. It is as though each generation of warriors lets the next generation turn its war into something it never was, acts of heroism and bonds of comradeship, the horror and the slaughter repressed and forgotten. War's great paradox is that we always turn it into an event where its brutal nature is obliterated by memories of heroism, comradeship, and glory.

Why do soldiers allow their war to be so purified? What is it about war that makes us lie when we tell of it? What is it we want to hide? And what envy lies in the souls of those men who never go to war? Is that why they must so glorify it? Declare its goodness? Because they were never there? Because they feel less sure of their manhood?

To ferret out the truth of war beyond these myths of the "Greatest Generation" is a difficult and, I think, even a dangerous task, for, in so doing it, one questions the most fundamental tenet of society: the basis for its patriotism. Required is the effort to examine with as much rigor as possible the literature of World War II, its memoirs, novels, and movies, searching for the true story of that war, what my generation really experienced. To understand what these books and films really show us of war, the stories they tell, to reject what appears to be false, accept what appears to be true, requires an effort that is likely to bring us to an understanding of World War II and the wars that have followed. That generation—my generation—which knew World War II's agonies and delights over sixty years ago, is dying at the rate of hundreds of thousands of men a year. Then who will be left to ensure that a just and accurate story is told and passed on to future generations of potential soldiers?

This is an effort almost never undertaken, almost as if the literature and movies of that war were sacrosanct, not to be criticized. Criteria for judging those efforts are required, criteria that must be painstakingly created: in spite of the enormous out-pouring of novels, memoirs, and movies telling us of that war, few critical standards for judging those works have been formed. Rather, interpretations of World War II are largely accepted at face value as if they were commandments. It is somehow considered wrong to judge stories told of war.

Memories of that past as it really happened must be rediscovered, the stories, events, and emotions forgotten and repressed over these long generations retold. In those remembrances of the way it really was, a clearer image of what my generation was truly like in the war is discovered: what acts it performed, what hopes it had, and what dreams it carried during the war and in that short time before war was declared to be "Good." In a world such as ours, with war still our preferred solution to foreign policy, with war conducted by weapons of such lethality, this is a task well-worth pursuing, a task essential to the future of our democracy.

~~∽~~

How can the generation born after World War II best judge the films and books—fiction and non-fiction—about that war, works pouring from the media today, a fountain of information interpreting and reinterpreting what was clearly the most important event of the last century, a media event that will surely continue far into this new century just as Civil War books and TV spectaculars appear a hundred and fifty years after that war that so changed the nation? As John Keegan, a military historian, has stated, there are no standards for judging the quality of battle novels and short stories: "The treatment of battle in fiction is a subject almost untouched by literary critics."[1] And, I would add, even less touched in film and the war memoir.

I have devoted the last twenty-seven years of my life to developing a critical framework for judging the art of World War II, reading war fiction, memoirs, and nonfiction, seeing movies, writing books about war, struggling always to develop reasonable criteria for such judgment that goes beyond myth, hero worship, comradeship, and glory, the usual standards for assessing the "goodness" of war-related art. Seeking such understanding, quite simply, has been a matter of life and death for me. My wounds shredded not only my body but also my emotions. I spent many, many years in recovery and, in fact, have never fully regained my equanimity. I had to understand war, what it was, what it did to me and to other men in battle if I myself were ever to come to terms with what happened to me at nineteen and, so, rediscover my sanity.

Out of that time in combat, those days and nights in the hospital, those memories of terror and confusion, gravel biting at my legs from exploding shells, machine gun fire as I crossed a broken bridge, mortar fire shredding the leaves above my head, men at my side slammed into the earth by shrapnel, blue holes of rifle fire punched into the night, the dead German soldier, younger than I, at my feet. . . . Out of that time, those years, I reached the conclusion that I had penetrated the darkest levels of the unconscious, places where men became animals, places no human should be asked to enter, the center of war a vast womb of silence, places of pitiless forces, dominated by death and killing's harsh mystery, places where soldiers became inarticulate, grunts, shouts, screams, ordinary words meaningless forms of expression in the chaos of terror in which they floundered.

This belief—no, this certainty—that war at its core is a place without pity, led me to a few simple and cogent questions that a work must answer in a meaningful and positive fashion if it is to be accepted as a successful and authentic rendering of battle. These questions become the criteria for judgment:

> ● Does the work of art—fiction, non-fiction, memoir, or film—give a sense of war's animal nature, a ruthless and mysterious place, the killing zone, where men live with the certainty of death?

● How is the act of killing treated? Is the haunting reality of imminent death or massive crippling from men's violence, the dismemberment of flesh, shown in all its brutality and finality? And does that destruction, in the deepest sense, resonate with the quality of overwhelming mystery, grief, pain, and anger that becomes almost a sacrament?

● Is the extraordinary complexity of human reaction to death and wounding, killing in combat, adequately presented beyond the clichés of courage and comradeship? Imminent death from violence in war puts many faces on the human being, ranging from the fiercest rage—"I'll get that sunuvabitch"—to a longing for flight, acts of betrayal, emotions of shame and guilt, sometimes cowardice, self-wounding, refusal to fire, skulking, firing into the air, combat exhaustion.

● What meaning is given to comradeship under fire? If real, how long does it last? Could the emotion of comradeship sometimes be mythical, the creation of a courageous reality to deny the insanity of killing, wounding, blood, body parts, death?

● Is the inane quality of dialogue in combat accepted so that action, internal monologue, and body language are given far greater weight than conversation, silence more important than speech?

● Do these complexities of war resonate through time far into the future, where their

real meaning is finally discerned in impacts
on future decades?

These questions have been helpful to me. They
may also help a generation that has never known
war reach some real understanding of the war their
fathers and grandfathers fought, the wars being
fought today, and the terror and complexity of war,
sometimes its majesty and mystery, even why some
men love it so. Two films, *Saving Private Ryan* and
The Thin Red Line and two authors of non-fiction
works—Stephen E. Ambrose and Tom Brokaw—
have, in recent years, attracted the greatest attention in the stunning revival of interest in World War
II. Since 1992, Ambrose has published *Band of Brothers, D-Day, Citizen Soldiers,* and *The Victors,* books
that have helped America define the role of the infantry in Europe in World War II. Tom Brokaw has
given us *The Greatest Generation* and its sequels, *The
Greatest Generation Speaks* and *An Album of Memories.* In 1999 *Saving Private Ryan* and *The Thin Red
Line* both received Oscar nominations. *Saving Private Ryan* won some awards; *The Thin Red Line,*
none.

Stephen Ambrose and Tom Brokaw tell us one
story about the American men who fought in World
War II, Steven Spielberg in *Saving Private Ryan,* a
second, and Terrence Malick and James Jones in *The
Thin Red Line,* both as movie and novel, a third. For
Ambrose and Brokaw the American men who fought
World War II were almost all heroes. Given a dirty
job they did it. Among those sixteen million service-
men and women there were few cowards, no betrayals, little shame or guilt, great comradeship.
Most remarkable is the manner in which they tell
us of those young men in battle. Both writers em-
ploy the words "kill" and "wound" over and over

again yet the reader never really senses the blood, never—is this the problem?—smells it, so sweet upon the air.

Ambrose is more sophisticated than Brokaw. He castigates the army for its replacement policy, and death is present, killing sometimes a haunted reality. Yet the reader senses that Ambrose is so struck with the "heroism" of the American combat infantryman, the "citizen soldier," that he refuses to penetrate the ruthless quality of the front, the pitiless place of the killing zone, to present the "combat numbness" of which James Jones writes so tellingly in his *The Thin Red Line*:

> A crazy sort of blood lust, like some sort of declared school holiday from all moral ethics, had descended on them. They could kill with impunity and they were doing it. . . . But John Bell, for one . . . could not help wondering if any of them could ever become the same again. He didn't think so. Not without lying, anyway. Perhaps long years after the war was done . . . they could pretend to each other that they were men. And avoid admitting that they had once seen something animal within themselves that terrified them. . . . So Doll had killed his first Japanese. For that matter his first human being of any kind. . . . Shooting well, at anything, was always a pleasure. And Doll hated the Japanese, dirty little yellow Jap bastards. . . . But beyond these two pleasures there was another. It had to do with guilt. . . . He had done the most horrible thing a human being could do, worse than rape even. And nobody in the whole damn world could say anything to him about it. . . . He had gotten by with murder.[2]

James Jones understands and shows us the animal nature of combat, the combat numbness that so destroys moral choice. He recognizes and explains the ease with which some American men learned to kill. Neither Ambrose nor Brokaw ever achieve his brutal honesty about the things the American soldier actually does in combat. Perhaps, never having been in combat themselves, they cannot grasp its dark meaning, a reality they mask with saccharine sentimentality.

Ambrose opposes Jones's reality with his faith in the "citizen soldier," the young American in his teens or early twenties who "stood to the test" and through courage and comradeship won the war, far from the Pacific Theater that so concerned Jones, the enemy there the "bestial Jap," allowing atrocities to be easily committed by the American soldier.

Other evidence beyond the work of James Jones raises the difficulties the American infantrymen faced in combat in World War II. In *America's Forgotten Army,* Charles Whiting writes that desertion in the European Theater was around forty thousand before Pvt. Eddie D. Slovik was executed for desertion on January 31, 1945.[3] Michael Doubler, writing in *Closing with the Enemy,* emphasized high levels of combat exhaustion: "The armies in Europe evacuated 151,920 cases of neuropsychiatric disorders to hospitals in 1944 and 1945, and combat units discovered that on average, for every three men killed or wounded, one other soldier became a psychiatric casualty."[4] Paul Fussell in *Wartime* points to the maximum combat time American psychiatrists believed a soldier could take, around 200 to 240 days.[5] Gerald F. Linderman in *The World Within War* indicates that some participants thought this number far too high: the limit could be reached in as few as twenty days or so.[6]

High turnover rates in frontline divisions, sometimes exceeding two hundred percent, desertions, combat fatigue, refusals to fire, each and all question the conclusions Ambrose and Brokaw reach. These harsh realities of war also make us pause when the claim of comradeship is put forward, particularly by Ambrose. Since illness, woundings, killings, and combat fatigue so decimate frontline troops, it is difficult—in fact impossible—to understand how the bonds of caring are maintained: the beloved comrade simply and suddenly disappears due to one of these causes, to be replaced by others who, in their turn, also vanish. Once seconded to the hospital, it is rare for the combat soldier to return to his unit and, if he does, that unit would now be irrevocably different from the one he left. The problem of the frontline soldier in World War II came down to survival in the harshest of realities where only peace, combat fatigue, wounding, self-wounding, or death marked the path to escape.[7]

Stephen Ambrose's emphasis on the courage and comradeship of the "citizen soldier" and Tom Brokaw's glorification of the "Greatest Generation" does little to help us understand what World War II was really all about. Paul Fussell in *Wartime* has stated: "America has not yet understood what the Second World War was like and has thus been unable to use such understanding to re-interpret and re-define the national reality and to arrive at something like public maturity."[8] Insights of far richer complexity and far greater sophistication than those of Ambrose and Brokaw are needed to reach that reinterpretation and maturity.

At war's end, Ambrose's and Brokaw's soldiers return to the United States, seemingly untouched by what they have seen and done in combat. They shut up, do not complain, and go about the business of building a new America. According to Ambrose:

> They had seen enough destruction; they wanted to construct. They built the Interstate Highway system, the St. Lawrence Seaway, the suburbs (so scorned by the sociologists, so successful with the people), and more. They had seen enough killing; they wanted to save lives. They licked polio and made other revolutionary advances in medicine. They had learned in the army the virtues of a solid organization and teamwork, and the value of individual initiative, inventiveness, and responsibility [This was scarcely the army I and my contemporaries experienced.] They developed the modern corporation while inaugurating revolutionary advances in technology, education, and public policy. . . . They supported NATO and the United Nations and the Department of Defense. They had helped stopped Hitler and Tojo. . . . They stopped Stalin and Krushchev."[9]

Brokaw clearly agrees. His "Greatest Generation" "helped convert a wartime economy into the most powerful peacetime economy in history. They made breakthroughs in medicine and other sciences. They gave the world new art and literature. They came to understand the need for federal civil rights legislation. They gave America Medicare."[10]

Of course, other conclusions can be drawn about the world created by American veterans since World War II. For many it has had disastrous impacts. The Friends Committee on National Legislation's *Washington Newsletter* reports that: "The U.S., with less than 5% of the world's population, consumes 25% of global oil production," in order to maintain its consumer economy.[11] We plunged into greed and glut after the war. Where else in the world can one buy five hundred dollar blue jeans, chose from forty brands of cereals, buy ten thousand dollar bottles of wines, build six thousand square foot houses, and drive SUVs that only get fifteen miles per gallon of gas? All this while children in Third World countries starve and die. Our vaunted technology leads to the destruction of the globe's air, water, earth, animals, fish, birds, insects, and has formed the mega-city, rife with urban sprawl, crime, violence, congestion, and pollution. Our unfair distribution of wealth creates a permanent underclass.

In the 1950s and 1960s, many of those who opposed the civil rights movement in the South were veterans who helped lynch, beat, and kill African Americans, often honorably discharged veterans themselves. One of the self-confessed murderers of Emmett Till was a veteran, "and a highly decorated one at that."[12] Veterans all—Eisenhower, Kennedy, Johnson, and Nixon—either initiated or led us deeper into the morass of the Vietnam War.

The quality of the America the veterans of World War II created has a far darker side than that proposed by Ambrose and Brokaw, one rooted in the sins of greed, gluttony, avarice, prejudice, and violence. In their cleaned-up stories, the GI is, in the oddest kind of way, so pure and so courageous he seems bloodless, with none of the animal nature of which Jones so movingly writes.

In his book about the Civil War, *Embattled Courage,* Gerald Linderman helps us understand the purification of memory, the startling change in the way combat is remembered by the veteran thirty years after the war. By the 1890s, service in the Civil War

had become the icon for political and economic success, the war sentimentalized into something it
never was, with fear, death, killing, wounding all
denied, repressed, forgotten.[13]

Siegfried Sassoon tells us the same story about
World War I:

"Song-Books of the War"

In fifty years, when peace outshines
Remembrance of the battle lines,
Adventurous lads will sigh and cast
Proud looks upon the plundered past.
On summer morn or winter's night,
Their hearts will kindle for the fight,
Reading a snatch of soldier-song,
Savage and jaunty, fierce and strong;
And through the angry marching rhymes
Of blind regret and haggard mirth,
They'll envy us the dazzling times
When sacrifice absolved our earth.

Some ancient man with silver locks
Will lift his weary head to say:
"War was a fiend who stopped our clocks
Although we met him grim and gay."
And then he'll speak of Haig's last drive,
Marveling that any came alive
Out of the shambles that men built
And smashed, to cleanse the world of guilt.
But the boys, with grin and sidelong glance,
Will think, "Poor grandad's day is done."
And dream of lads who fought in France
And lived in time to share the fun.[14]

Ambrose and Brokaw pursue this same falsifi-
cation of memory. The generation that follows the

war generation apparently must turn their father's war into a neater, cleaner experience than the pitiless place that lies at the heart of battle.

Not so with parts of *Saving Private Ryan.* Spielberg's war resonates in contrast to the wars of Ambrose and Brokaw. The soldier shown to come home in the film is Private Ryan himself—to a life that must have been so painful that, at the end of the film, he asks his wife if he had been a "good man." Private Ryan's life must have been haunted, night and day, by the memory of the men who died to give him a chance. War—with me, with Private Ryan, with James Jones, with, I believe, all men who survive serious combat—always shadows the future. Spielberg's film is to be given the highest marks for his grasp of war's resonance over time.

The film otherwise, though, does not rise to such high benchmarks. Spielberg's war is noisy, literally bursting with sound, from the invasion on Omaha Beach to the final firefight at the bridge. The silence of battle is what I remember most: tanks fired ten feet from me and I do not recall a sound. The silence of war, its terrible isolation and loneliness, is lost amidst the loud rattle of the film. Moreover, the fact of death and killing slips away. What Spielberg offers instead is a war of loud and murderous firepower—incessant gunfire—and a place where men talk too much in sentences unlikely to be formulated in the heat of battle.

In my experience, men near death are quiet, quiet and alone, for words cannot bridge such distance. Perhaps a touch, an embrace, tears, sobs, but not words. Articulate language is too sophisticated for the facts of death and the emotions that throb with killing. Though, to be fair, Spielberg renders many scenes with a realism laced with brutal irony, but always missing is that aura of silence that so dominates the place of killing where spirits of those just killed seem to writhe through the air, spirits of the dead and dying, the pain they leave behind them in this ominous, brooding place of terror.

The Thin Red Line, from its opening scene to its conclusion, dwells in that place of death where strange and wondrous events occur, mystery, even majesty, a darkness that verges on the beautiful. In this film, men talk but seldom to each other; rather they ruminate or hear voices about this place of war they have come to inhabit. In Malick's take, the beauty of the natural world—and its destructive capacity—is forcefully shown: the silent wind sweeping over the fields of grass in fading summer sun, men dying in those fields of fire, nature and men juxtaposed in the rage of war to give a sense of evil, a personification of the evil in the human soul. That darkness is shown in a way that breaks the heart: Lieutenant Colonel Tall driving his soldiers so he can obtain his full colonel's eagle, the corporal extracting gold teeth from dead Japanese—these scenes reveal a darkness as brutally realistic as Saving Private Ryan.

But Spielberg's film, though visually realistic, reinforces those clichés we learn from Ambrose and Brokaw, those visions of heroism and glory so derided by Hemingway—portraits of sentimental comradeship and bravery. Saving Private Ryan is, finally, a Hollywood concoction, having little to do with the reality of World War II in its most fundamental meaning. Malick's art offers the mystery, the poetry, and the pain, which always lies at war's hard core. For me The Thin Red Line excels because it comes from the best fiction about World War II, James Jones's novel by the same name.

In his novel, Jones depicts an infantry company in combat, a hundred and fifty men dealing with their essences and who they are as humans in the terrible center of war. A few of these soldiers are courageous, some cowards, some murderous, some cruel, some kind, most doing what they have to do. But most seem multidimensional and marked forever by their experience. They are real, not figures of literary concoction or irony. They are men changed by war. And perhaps it is this fact of being crippled in ways they cannot articulate that makes both the novel and the film much more powerful than most other attempts to deal artistically with World War II. Some of us may have come back like the heroes Ambrose and Brokaw describe, but most of us never fully recovered, never became the men we might have been, a part of us lost forever in the world of combat where we discovered truths about ourselves that changed us in ways we never fully understood.

The generation born after World War II has a choice of stories it can use to understand and interpret the war its fathers and grandfathers fought. It can select the tales of Ambrose and Brokaw, the "hero," the man unafraid in war, surrounded by comrades, competent in war, competent in peace. It can follow Spielberg's veteran, haunted forever by what he saw and did, war never all it seems, but a place of irony, of hidden truths, sudden turns, haunted by the most brutal realism. Or, with Jones and Malick, it can search that brutalism for powerful statements of good and evil, for acts of violence intimate to the human and natural world, even visions of beauty born out of conflict, discovering a place of mysterious and terrible silence which lies at the core of life, all we ever know of the worst—and sometimes the best—that men may ever be. It is in this vision of war that war's deepest meaning may be discovered.

The story a generation elects to tell about the war of its fathers may determine the nature of the war that it and its children fight. The story this new generation has elected to pass on is the combination of the tales of Ambrose and Brokaw, the courage and comradeship of the "citizen soldier," the stoicism and bravery of the "Greatest Generation" at times mixed with the realism and irony of Steven Spielberg. The meaning of *The Thin Red Line* as film or novel has slowly disappeared over time, too uncomfortable a tale for a generation bred outside of war and the mystery of death and killing and wounding at war's core, that pitiless place from where men never return the same. This is not the story that men and women of today's generation want to hear.

Rather, the story told in the mainline media explains why it was so easy for America to accept the idea of a "war on terror." Once again, we would storm the beaches of Normandy. Once again we would bomb the people of Japan. Our policies of preemption, our war with Iraq are rooted in a war now sixty years past. By believing the Myths of World War II as the truth of war we have but created another monstrosity, resembling our failure in Vietnam, another war that will only cripple those who fight it, harm our armed forces, erode our reputation throughout the world, and, this time, turn much of the world against us.

CHAPTER 5

The World War II Memoir

Another type of literature that forms the collective image of World War II is the war memoir. Since 1945, thousands have been published. Which are reliable? Which lie? Which gloss over that pitiless place at the heart of war? These are questions seldom asked, except sometimes by a reviewer of the memoir. A war memoir, even more than the war movie or the war novel, seems to have something sacrosanct about it. It is not to be questioned.

For this reason, discovering criteria for judging the war memoir of World War II is a most difficult task. I have long puzzled over the reason for this dilemma, reading as many of these memoirs as possible since I was wounded in that war. My conclusion is that criticism of a memoir or books based on memoirs verges on bad manners, a crude invasion into the character and honesty of another life. The writer has already bargained his life for his story. Who gives me the right, who gives anyone the right to come along and judge another combatant's version of war?

And, yet, now, I have come to believe that such criticism and judgment, as sensitive, as difficult as they are, are essential. World War II was the most terrible event of the twentieth century. It changed the world in ways we have yet to completely understand. To grasp the meaning of that war so that we can effectively prevent other wars, or at least diminish their horror, means we must search for all that is true about that war while rejecting all that is false.

~◈~

My interest in developing criteria for judging the validity of the war memoir arises from the struggle I had in writing the truth about my experiences in combat in World War II.[1] Though my narrative of that day and night and day again in battle takes up but one chapter in my memoir, the rest of the book being devoted to causes of the war and its consequences on my personal life, that one chapter was far harder to write than all of the rest. Completing it took over four or five years and as many as thirty or forty rewrites to reach what I could accept as the truth. And even now I am not absolutely sure about that truth.

Dealing with those truths about myself in combat, truths I was afraid to divulge even to myself, was a process that took me through a trajectory of rage, then bitterness, followed by repression for decades, finally slow recovery of memories deeply buried for so long. It was only when I returned to the place of my wounding that I could begin to confront all I really had experienced, those facts of fear and anger, loneliness and alienation, guilt and shame, memories locked deep within.

Writing of them was traumatic. Most of all I had to face my fear that I had been a coward at the front. For long decades I ran from my inner condemnation of myself, of all I was supposed to be as a man.

I feared this because I had been at the front for only a day and a half, because no one had spoken to me, given me a word of advice or friendship, because I was totally alone, because I was terrified. I had fired only one shot in combat and that into the fog of war. I felt—no, I knew—I had failed at the greatest test a man may ever have. I repressed that harsh judgment of myself and that repression nearly destroyed me. I ran to a foreign country, tried to write about war but failed, unable to face what I believed was my lack of manhood. When I returned to the States, I had no career, and, when I finally put myself together again, I repressed for decades all memories of the war.

My return to the French battlefield in 1984 freed me in the most wonderful and creative way. It let me understand, at last, that what I had done was enter the cauldron of combat totally alone, a boy of nineteen, without friends or comrades, yet stand up to the test and do what I was told to do, my "duty." It let me understand that my wounding was the result of the army's brutal "replacement policy." In 1944, after the invasion of France, the need for replacements skyrocketed. To meet that need, ill-trained young men, mostly boys like myself, were thrown into combat, their casualty rate predictably catastrophic. Most of all, returning to the place of wounding freed me to write of war and its impact on my life. I could finally put on paper what I knew to be the truth of combat.

The sentence in the first chapter of my memoir, *On Being Wounded*, spoken by the lieutenant as the stretcher-bearers slid me into the ambulance—"You didn't like it much up here, did you, Wood?"—gave me great agony in recalling that past, and then writing of it. His words—no, his judgment of me—contained the harshest truth about myself, one I didn't even want to admit to my own consciousness: I hadn't liked combat, had done nothing heroic, simply done what I was told to do. I hadn't even shot anyone, only got hit myself. I was ashamed. I asked myself: Had I been a man? Had I been a coward? What did the lieutenant's question say about myself, about his observation of my acts?

I harrowed myself with such questions until I returned to the place of wounding, discovering my acts were actually ones of great courage: a replacement into the Seventh Armored Division, without a word of support, I did do as I was told to, in moments when I conquered fear, though so alone, under fire.

But to put the lieutenant's judgment of me into print, my fears naked to the world, how could I do that? I still writhe inside when I read his words. But, maybe his question gets to the core of who I was at nineteen and who I have become: I don't like war. I didn't like war. Further, my conclusion is that most men who fight don't like war.

I had the responsibility to tell what I believed to be true even when it made me extremely uncomfortable. Struggling with this one wrenching issue, revealing truths about myself I considered unpleasant, even unmanly, finally able even to write them for the general public, has driven me on my continuing search for criteria for judging the reliability and the truth of the war memoir of World War II. I have asked myself countless times how well I told the story of my time in combat, how close I came to the truth of men seeking to kill each other, hard steel ripping soft flesh, the terror that accompanies duty at the front in war, that place without pity. I simply don't know the answer to my question. I know I struggled to be as honest as I could.

I also knew that to be honest the tale of combat must involve far more than just the experiences of men in battle. For me, two events involving civilians after the liberation of a town in eastern France made me know that war's impact on non-combatants was as important to the truth of war as the story of the infantryman. Some of the town's residents, I was told, had been imprisoned in a slave labor camp where men and women had been forced to work in coal and iron mines for four long years, without proper food or housing or medical care. That night as we heard their shouts, felt the heat of their joy as they pressed upon our half-track, I felt like a giant, ten feet tall: we, American soldiers, had freed these people from their Nazi rulers. Their joy gave me some understanding of their long years of pain. Yet, the next morning, I watched the down side of liberation as an angry crowd found a scapegoat, a young woman who had been a "horizontal" collaborator. They put her on a platform, stripped her, cut her hair to her scalp. I sensed the hard rage of the crowd before her, muttered curses, the anger that also comes with liberation, the need to find the cause of the pain and punish it. Watching the anguish of that woman as men and women, freed slave laborers, her neighbors, former friends, perhaps former lovers, mocked her, exposed me to another kind of horror at the root of war. It struck down civilians as much as the artillery fire when it hit our squad, as much as the wet slap of shrapnel did when it ripped into a soldier's flesh.

How combat impacted civilians, usually innocents, women, children, old folks, was as important to the truth of war as that of men in battle, a part of the tale usually neglected in the telling of war stories.

And yet, even with this understanding, achieving reliability in my memoir still remained difficult. Later in life, as I fell asleep, I could see our half-track paused on the macadam road at my side, its motor growling as our squad of infantrymen clung to its safety. The company captain stands next to me. A hundred yards or so down the road, a group of German soldiers stagger out of the woods at the edge of the road, their hands in the air, screaming *Komrade! Komrade!*

The captain, the tightest little smile on his face, orders the sergeant behind the .50-caliber machine on the top of the track, "Shoot those sunsabitches. I want 'em dead. Dead. Dead." The gunner shakes his head. The captain orders him to fire again. The gunner starts to refuse. The captain reaches down toward the .45-caliber pistol strapped to his hip. Suddenly, with a sharp, abrupt motion of anger, the gunner lowers his barrel. A harsh rap of fire slams into the fleeing Germans who sprawl over the pavement, cut to pieces by .50-caliber rounds.

The memory ends. Was it true? Or was it a concoction of movies, novels, and other memoirs I had seen and read? I don't know. And I will never know. But, finally, I decided not to include it in my memoir. Too uncertain of its truth, it smelt of the sharp odor of the spectacular, too much a movie scene. It also told a terrible story about another man, one I could never verify. My memoir did not need to rest on such uncertainties to present the truth of war.

Struggling to clarify the truth of my time in combat so as to write clearly about it always remained a task of enormous complexity, demanding many, many drafts. There is a scene in the book in which I fire an M-1 rifle into a fog of smoke as the bridge over the Moselle River is blown up by the Germans. I remember the stick figures of Germans running several hundred yards away just before the explosion. I remember dropping the canister of machine gun ammunition I carried and throwing my rifle butt to my shoulder. But, for the life of me, I cannot re-member whether I actually fired or not when the pall of smoke fell over the fleeing Germans. It is amazing but the memory is gone. Completely gone. I finally wrote that I fired into the drifting smoke. Am I one hundred percent sure? No.

I based my conclusion that I probably had fired on the fact that I had grown up with guns, shot .22s beginning at ten or twelve years of age, then shot-guns for rabbits, squirrel, quail, and pheasants. I don't believe I would have lifted a rifle to my shoul-der, aimed, finger on the trigger, and not fired, par-ticularly with a round in the chamber. It would have been automatic, second nature.

If it was difficult to remember the truth in com-bat experiences such as those, and then write about it, when I came to the memories around which most memoirs are formed—the heroism attributed to sol-diers and the warmth of comradeship at the front—I sank deeply into even greater problems, even more complex to manage.

In one scene in the book my squad has stumbled from the half-track and cautiously sneaks around a curve of the road. Suddenly, a flat plain spreads before us, in the distance the arch of a bridge over the Moselle River. The squad suddenly realizes that it is at the front of the whole U.S. Third Army. I wrote and rewrote this scene many, many times, knowing I had put some falsity within it. Finally, I discovered my error: I had unconsciously placed myself at the front of the squad, the sacrificial "goat," the replacement who would draw fire. It simply wasn't true. I was never at the head of the squad, probably too damned scared. I brought up the rear, lugging an ammunition canister for the light .30-cali-ber machine gun. I had tried to inflate myself into something I never was, the soldier at the forefront of the war, leading his "buddies" into combat, the unpraised "hero" who would save his squad. The whole scene was a lie until I put myself at the back of the squad.

But struggling to write the scene's truth told me how much I had longed to be part of that squad, how much I missed my buddies when I reached the front. When we arrived in England as replacements, most of us who had been together for many months were split up. In France we were divided even further, some of us put into a two-and-a-half ton truck carrying twenty or thirty replacements to the Seventh Armored Division. Once we reached the division we were separated again. Only two replacements, myself and another private I had never seen before, were sent to our company. The company scarcely welcomed us. We received no orientation, no training, only harsh looks, thrown into the line the next morning, yelled at for our mistakes. Front line friendship, companionship—a joke.

These soldiers had trained together for over two years and served in combat for less than three weeks. I was probably the first replacement thrown into their midst, replacing God only knows who—a friend of years perhaps, a man wounded or killed. The last thing they wanted to do was welcome the stranger into their midst when they weren't even yet confident of what they were doing in war, still so new themselves to battle's chaos, frightened of the dumb acts a replacement could commit that might get them killed. To make it all even gloomier, after I was wounded I was dropped by the stretcher-bearers under fire, left to lie while artillery rounds continued to explode around me. I could even see the stretcher-bearers, safe from shrapnel in their refuge from artillery fire. Then the lieutenant's words!

I never experienced one instant of the vaunted

comradeship of which so many memoirs speak as the major value of combat at the front. For me, battle brought enormous alienation from humanity, an intense fear of annihilation. Only when I reached the battalion aid station, then the field hospital, did I sense that caring and comradeship I so longed for but never received in my unit.

~~~

Out of that long effort at writing my own memoir, two-plus decades of searching for the truth of my time in combat, and my long discipline of reading as many other memoirs as I could, I have finally been able to derive two preliminary criteria for judging the war memoir. I offer them as but a first step in thinking through one of the most troublesome problems of war literature: how do we determine the "reliability" of a war memoir?

For me, the most important of all considerations, the first criterion for determining that honesty, lies in a revelation presented by Fyodor Dostoyevsky in *Notes from the Underground*: "In every man's memory there are things he won't reveal to others, except, perhaps, to friends. And there are things he won't reveal even to friends, only, perhaps, to himself, and then, too, in secret. And finally, there are things he is afraid to reveal even to himself. . . ."[2]

In writing of battle, does the writer struggle with those facts of his combat experience far below consciousness, conditions and memories that have haunted him since his time in battle, realities he might not even understand but seeks to give some form and shape in words? Combat is probably the most intense experience men ever have. In it, more than any other place in life, they discover who they truly are. They face horrendous conditions of killing and dying, being hurt in a place without mercy, reduced to the nature of the animal. Soldiers are forced to exist in the depths of hell and discover how they function there.

As I struggled to understand the nature of my combat experience and read about the experience of others, I came to the conclusion that in the place of combat every man learns something about himself he would rather not know, shaming him. It can be anything: fear of such proportion that he cannot function; a desire to skulk; betrayal of a comrade; refusal to fire; sometimes even that he enjoyed the killing. It makes no difference the discovery. This is the human fact of which Dostoyevsky writes; there are events we cannot even tell ourselves about ourselves.

Those memoirs I trust most are those in which the author attempts to tell us of events he scarcely understands, scarcely wishes to reveal about himself. In Paul Fussell's *Doing Battle,* there is the innate distrust of all he experienced as an infantry officer in World War II, a kind of inward revulsion toward the whole, horrible mess that changed his life forever. Eugene Sledge tells us of his hard experiences as a Marine in combat in *With the Old Breed*, fellow Marines at the end of a long line, barely holding hands while dangling over a precipice. William Manchester reveals his last harrowing days of combat on the islands of the South Pacific in *Goodbye Darkness*. Raymond Gantter describes in *Roll Me Over* how American officers, victorious in war in 1945, occupying Germany, fat off the black market, used German women for their pleasure in ways that avoided the charge of rape. J. Glenn Gray in *The Warriors* deals with those who enjoy war, with the emotion of guilt. Howard Zinn, in *On War*, criticizes the bombing of Royan, France, by the United States in April 1945, an air raid that was unnecessary but in which he participated. It is memoirs such as these that plunge into the dark heart of the soldier at war that lead me toward war's truth.[3]

A second criterion I have finally been able to firmly establish comes from asking: how close does the writer come to war's horror? Do we shudder when we read his story? Do we see the impact of war on innocents?

When I think of this criterion, I remember another kind of war story, not the endless stories of days in combat, heroism and comradeship, but the memoirs of the forgotten, those in the Resistance in France and the rest of the Europe, men and women who fought a silent war, most often alone, many times ending before a firing squad or worse, in a cell, their bodies destroyed by Nazi or Milice brutes. I think most often of Jean Moulin and his memoir, *Premier Combat,* his first struggle against the Germans in 1940.[4] I think of his courage, fleeing to England to stand by de Gaulle, then back to France to organize the pieces of the Resistance into a coherent whole. I think of the stories told of him in his last days, tortured to death by Klaus Barbie and his Gestapo cohorts in Lyon, France, in 1944.[5]

Memoirs meeting these two criteria—plunging into the darkness of the self, presenting the horror of war—come closest in their power to Wilfred Owens's *Dulce et Decorum Est*, one of the best pieces written in the twentieth century about the reality of combat.[6]

> Bent double, like old beggars under sacks,
> Knock-kneed, coughing like hags, we cursed
>   through sludge,
> Till on the haunting flares we turned our backs
> And towards our distant rest began to trudge.

Men marched asleep. Many had lost their boots
But limped on, blood-shod. All went lame; all
    blind;
Drunk with fatigue; deaf even to the hoots
Of tired, outstripped Five-Nines that dropped
    behind.

Gas! Gas! Quick, boys!—An ecstasy of fumbling,
Fitting the clumsy helmets just in time;
But someone still was yelling out and stumbling
And flound'ring like a man in fire or lime . . .
Dim, through the misty panes and thick green
    light,
As under a green sea, I saw him drowning.

In all my dreams, before my helpless sight,
He plunges at me, guttering, choking, drowning.

If in some smothering dreams you too could
    pace
Behind the wagon that we flung him in,
And watch the white eyes writhing in his face,
His hanging face, like a devil's sick of sin;
If you could hear, at every jolt, the blood
Come gargling from the froth-corrupted lungs,
Obscene as cancer, bitter as the cud
Of vile, incurable sores on innocent tongues,—
My friend, you would not tell with such high
    zest
To children ardent for some desperate glory,
The old Lie: Dulce et decorum est
Pro patria mori.*

Memoirs that approach the poems of Wilfred
Owens, that dare speak war's harsh truth, some-

---

*It is sweet and right to die for your country.

times even have faint echoes of Homer's *The Iliad,*
clearly the most superb treatment of the agony of
combat ever written. But most memoirs never
seem to approach such honesty. It seems to me
they become bogged down in the difficulties I had
in writing my memoir: first and most essential—
did the event really happen? Or was it a concoction made from old memories, sweetened by books
read and movies seen, by the Myths of World
War II?

I marvel at some of the memoirs I read: how
does the author remember so much? In my memoir
I had such enormous difficulty reconstructing a day,
a night, a day. Some of these writers appear to remember every day and everything that happened to
them on that day. When they go on and on, span-
ning months of combat, my hackles of suspicion
begin to rise: could all they write of really have happened? Why do so few writers of war memoirs pause
and question their past, ask if their memory has
played them false?

When I read memoirs that emphasize those
combat experiences that gave me such difficulty—
heroism and comradeship—I begin to wonder if the
author has simply forgotten what really happened or,
if he does remember, must deny it, as Dostoyevsky
intimates, to maintain his inward integrity. To admit the truth of what he really did in the war, the
killing, the pain, the agony, his part in the horror,
all that really happens at the front, its animal nature, simply might destroy all sense of himself, the
self formed while living a comfortable, civilian life
after leaving combat. I wonder why memoirs never
are written by those who deserted, who ran black
markets, raped, skulked, refused to fire, were cowards, ran from fire, were replacements such as
myself, terribly wounded after a few days of utter

isolation at the front, even more telling, written by men who enjoyed the killing, even reveled in it. I wonder, always, if there is some truth about himself the writer of most memoirs denies: a truth, whatever it is, that shreds his image of himself as a man, the truth of which Dostoyevsky speaks, the horror which Jean Moulin knew. Rather than face that truth and admit it publicly, it is masked, hidden, finally so denied it is no longer conscious and, so, begins to taint his whole story of war.

I wonder if this is why so many memoirs fall into clichés of heroism and bravery and comradeship. The story told must become something other than it was so as to deny unadmitted truths, truths masked now by myths that cover up human failure, and the shame of war. The story, as time passes, begins to put courage, comradeship, and heroism, the highest qualities of the human being, at the core of the combat experience: if the truth about oneself cannot be admitted, then, clearly, it cannot be raised about others.

So I ask myself again and again: how reliable is the war memoir? How can we judge that reliability?

~∾~

I have found that some other writers about World War II also struggle with the problem of the reliability of the war memoir as part of American life: Paul Fussell, Howard Zinn, Samuel Hynes, Gerald Linderman, Richard Holmes, Patrick O'Donnell. Fussell's writing was the first I read that related to the questions I was beginning to ask about the memoirs of World War II after I had written my own. Fussell carefully and completely poked holes in the "Good War" and the "Greatest Generation." His whole book *The Great War and*

Modern Memory centered on the way World War I was remembered, how its myths changed our world. It helped me understand the powerful force of the myths of war in America that followed World War II. Zinn taught me that behind America's worship of those myths of war as expressed in so many memoirs existed another reality, our search for ways of peace. Seldom reported, seldom taught, this longing for a peaceful world was crucial to an understanding of our past, ways of thinking and feeling so neglected in most memoirs. Hynes devoted the first chapter of his book to the validity of the stories men tell of war. He respects those memoirs that "bear witness," reflecting my concern for revelations of the truth about oneself in the midst of the horror of war. Linderman presents the problem of the "purification of memory" in the last chapter of both of his books, war remembered as courage and comradeship. He points toward those areas where I had such difficulty in writing my memoir: the repression of years, the heroic fallacy, comradeship. Holmes devotes several pages to the difficulties of writing the war memoir. He raises basic problems of this form of literature: the limited experience, the "tunnel vision" of any combat soldier, the way memory plays tricks, the need to make a story out of something that simply may not be a story. O'Donnell, who collects oral history, points to problems of verification.[7]

Their observations are supported by writers in other cultures. Siegfried Sassoon's *Song-Books of the War* made the case for England. George L. Mosse points to the same process in Europe after World War I, particularly in Germany where he writes that "the Myth of the War Experience was central to the process of brutalization because it had transformed the memory of war and made it acceptable, providing nationalism with some of its most effective post-war myths and symbols."[8] Memoirs in Germany both immediately after the war and later provided the support for this myth.[9]

It is as if in all modern countries that experience the horror of industrial warfare the same type of memoir has to be written about war, masking what really happened, inventing another story, and building upon the myths of heroism and comradeship. The brutality of modern war must be denied, the wrenching rending of flesh by so much steel, whether in combatant or civilian. War becomes a form of glory. Those who fight it are great, those who die in it, even greater. Killing and being killed become pathways to a treasured eternity. All reality must be hidden.

And this is why, in this country, some writers, most of all Steven Ambrose and Tom Brokaw, succeed so well, using the war memoir as they do to praise the "citizen soldier" and the "Greatest Generation." They never really get to the level of killing in industrial warfare, what it really is like, and the impersonal pain. They don't appear to question any of the war stories they are told, to wonder about "purification of memory" (or if they do so, quickly brush the concern aside). The limited vision of the individual combat soldier in warfare, how stories are so often created out of unrelated events to make sense of what has no sense, never seems to bother them. They rely on the human need to give the horror of combat qualities of heroism and comradeship, thus masking what really happens. They seem to have accepted whole cloth the stories told to them after the war, the American soldier now somehow a little god, beyond the pain described in memoirs that hit closer to home: those of Fussell, Sledge, Manchester, Gantter, Gray, and Zinn.

If we are ever to learn to live without weapons and enemies, it is memoirs by men (and women now) who have been trapped by the war machine and who are willing to reveal the truth about themselves within its grasp that we must learn to trust. These are men and women who avoid the clichés of comradeship and courage, men and women who struggle to remember what really happened to them in their time at the front. As long as our interpretation of war rises from memoirs that mask truths the writer cannot admit, turning combat into a place only of heroism, not of pain, only of comradeship, not of alienation, our centuries-old dedication to the fields of war will never be changed and new generations will continue to long for fields of glory that never really existed, glories invented to deny war's hard and bitter truths.

The nature and quality of modern war, its impersonal mechanization, the ease with which we declare war, send our troops into battle, and accept the morally reprehensible killing of innocents at a distance or up close by our young men and women, all these demand we judge the war memoir more harshly than at any moment in its long history. This becomes especially true today as we become more wedded to the Myths of World War II, more apt to use them, without criticism, while reading the newest memoirs bound to follow our excursions into Afghanistan and Iraq.

CHAPTER 6

The World War II Novel

Rereading the war novels of World War II I have always admired most—the James Jones trilogy *From Here to Eternity, The Thin Red Line,* and *Whistle*; Norman Mailer's *The Naked and the Dead*; Irwin Shaw's *The Young Lions*; Robert Bowen's *The Weight of the Cross*; Kurt Vonnegut's *Slaughterhouse Five*; and Joseph Heller's *Catch 22*—has brought back lessons from that war we have forgotten. Warnings about America are given in these novels—the terrible stresses and dangers of war, what America was and what it might become—warnings that have gone unheeded for over fifty years. War is described as tragedy and madness, as the source of a brutal authoritarianism and corruption with fascism expected as a consequence of the war. The leaders of the military were often seen as more than willing to sacrifice their men and American civil liberties in order to reach their goals of worldwide victory.

All the heroes of these novels are ravaged by the war in a variety of ways. Some are tragic figures, destroyed by external fate or a tragic flaw within. A very few of these, in spite of the harshest combat and cruelest authority, often leading to their death, manage to preserve some sense of nobility and pride to the end. But many collapse under those same conditions. Some show an insatiable need for power. The crudest anti-Semitism occasionally strikes. Cowardice appears. Favors are sold and bribes taken. A wicked sense of satire often prevails.

In James Jones' three novels, the main characters are shadowed by a sense of inevitable doom and always are defeated. Though the names change in each novel, Jones essentially carries the same person forward. For example, as Jones indicates in his introductory note to *Whistle*, Private Prewitt in the first book becomes Private Witt in the second and Private Prell in the third. First Sergeant Warden and Mess Sergeant Stark undergo similar transitions. Following the recurring characters, the reader is overwhelmed by the destruction that they experience. Prewitt is persecuted by the officers and non-commissioned jocks in his company, falsely placed in the stockade where he witnesses a murder, tries to avenge that murder, is knifed, and finally is killed after he attempts to return to his company. In the final book, Private Prell, a Medal of Honor winner, is killed in a senseless barroom brawl instigated by his own rage and guilt. First Sergeant Warden/Welsh/Winch survives the first two books though he slowly sinks into his own madness, ending in book three in the psychiatric ward of a base hospital. And Mess Sergeant Stark/Storm/Strange commits suicide by jumping into the Atlantic Ocean from the deck of a troop ship en route to Europe in early summer 1944 as he returns to combat after having been wounded in the Pacific Theater.

Thus, all of Jones's main characters are crippled in some way. Further, the American society to which they return is crippled as well. Men and women are unable to reach stable and loving relationships. They are mired in a constant, even crazy, pursuit of orgasm and "going down" on each other as if the creation of children and family were some kind of perversion, normality totally lost for men returned from combat and, now, the women they chase.

In *The Naked and the Dead*, Lieutenant Hearn, aide to Maj. Gen. Edward Cummings, rebels against the authority of the general. Transferred into a combat platoon, he is killed. Noah Ackerman in *The Young Lions* is treated brutally by the captain and many of the men in his platoon because he is Jewish. Having evolved into the most decent person in the book, he is killed in the last chapter by a corrupt German soldier, leaving a young wife and a child behind, never fulfilling his promise as a poet. Two sailors—Gaddy and Tom—carry the burden of *The Weight of the Cross.* Gaddy degenerates into a psychopath while Tom survives as a decent human being, stripped of all the burdens of his past but only after he has released his angry memories through an act of killing.

Kurt Vonnegut reflects on the insanity of the war in *Slaughterhouse Five.* Present in the book as the narrator, he is overwhelmed by the incomprehensible destruction of Dresden by British and American bombers. The war is so brutal with the killing of thousands of innocents that the only way Vonnegut makes sense of the madness of war as a writer is to create the science-fiction world of Tralfamadore. Yossarian in Heller's *Catch 22* struggles to escape the war after living with the craziness and corruption of his fellow officers, but, in the deepest sense, his escape is another form of madness, as he decides to flee to Sweden in the midst of the war. Both these last two books give a sense of a deranged world, the killings incomprehensible in any normal frame. The only way to speak of war is through bitter satire and fantasy.

Given that all the best novelists of World War II saw the soldier as either damaged or corrupted and the war as a time of brutal madness, the most fascinating comment we can make today is how this understanding has long since disappeared completely, at least in America. World War II is not thought of as tragic, corrupt, or insane; rather most people think of it today as that time when the "Greatest Generation" bravely did its duty—and this stuns me—at no or little cost! We have sanitized the war to the point that it is no longer dirty, obscene, or even really dangerous. Instead it is remembered as a time of opportunity for courage and honor, the chance to prove one's manhood. The predictions of Siegfried Sassoon in *Song-Books of the War* have come back full force to haunt us in this Second World War.

Nothing changes. War is always glorified and its reality neglected or forgotten.

~⹀~

It is also clear that at least three of the novelists—Jones, Mailer, and Bowen—saw the war for what it was, a working class war. Their heroes are, in their terms, "working class stiffs." They deal with the forgotten fact that in World War II the army often sent those with lower scores on placement tests into infantry divisions.[1]

These novelists spoke a truth almost completely forgotten today, a truth best expressed by Eugene Debs, the Socialist Party candidate for president in 1916. Although receiving over 900,000 votes for president, in 1917 Debs was arrested and later sentenced to ten years in prison for a speech that concluded with this anti-war statement: "The master class has always declared the wars; the subject class has always fought the battles. The master class has had all to gain and nothing to lose; the subject class has nothing to gain and all to lose—especially their lives."[2]

~~~

In *The Naked and the Dead,* General Cummings says, "This is going to be the reactionary's century, perhaps their thousand-year reign. It's the one thing Hitler said which wasn't completely hysterical. . . . After the war our foreign policy is going to be far more naked, far less hypocritical than it has ever been. We're no longer going to cover our eyes with our left hand while our right is extending an imperialist paw."[3]

Catch 22 and James Jones's trilogy support this thesis of Norman Mailer, the potential for fascism in the United States following the war. The officer class in all these novels is, quite simply, corrupt in the deepest sense. The officers in *Catch 22* sell American services to Germans, do anything to make a buck, have absolutely no sense of the meaning of the democracy for which they fight. The officers in Jones's novels are poisoned by power: they destroy Prewitt, who refuses to box in the regimental boxing match; Lieutenant Colonel Tall drives his men beyond their capacity to assure his colonel's eagle. In *The Naked and the Dead*, General Cummings is the instrument of Hearn's death, assigning him to a combat platoon.

In fact, Mailer was more certain of the potential of an authoritarian state in America's future than any of the other novelists. Both his leaders, General Cummings and Sergeant Croft, are egocentric bullies, caring only for their own power, contemptuous of democratic values, careless of the men for whom they are responsible. These men Mailer saw as the future leaders of America.

How accurate were such predictions? It is not likely that any of these writers expected the revolution in civil liberties that has swept through the country since the end of World War II. Blacks can now vote and cannot legally be prevented from living where they please. Women have opportunities unknown in 1945, not just in work but in the right to control their bodies. Gays have less need to hide and are beginning to be protected against discrimination (outside the military). The handicapped have come into their own. An explosion of freedom has occurred in the United States.

But, in the area of political rights, freedom has been constrained. Both in the McCarthy era in the Cold War against the communists and today in the war against terrorism, the federal government exhibits the need to repress those with unpopular opinions deemed "dangerous" to the nation and to eavesdrop on private conversations. Mailer, Heller, and Jones point to a continuing trend in American political practice: the desire to repress the rebel, the recalcitrant, the individualist, to offer freedom only to those who collaborate with central power.

~∾~

Thus the novelists of World War II offer us considerable insights into both the nature of war and the nature of ourselves as Americans. All of them saw World War II exactly for what it was—a dirty, dangerous business that destroyed the best of the nation. They know that the infantrymen's lot is tragic, a fate beyond control. Some of them recognize that there is a deep authoritarian streak in American political practice, one that is always present, dangerous to our democracy, one that must be challenged by a better sense of what the First Amendment and freedom really mean. And some of them go even further, showing war to be the insane asylum it really is.

Are these dangers of which we must be aware as we heedlessly rush forward in a war with terrorists for which there is seemingly no end?

CHAPTER 7

An Opportunity Lost

For a few moments after it ended, World War II was remembered as it really was, before its myths clouded its harsh reality. Only a few of us still alive remember those brief, magical times when the world and its nations resonated with the hope for a better and more peaceful world. For a short time so many of us lived and dreamed that hope. We had seen a world destroyed. Some of us had killed, some of us had been wounded; all of us had lost friends. We had helped smash towns and cities, watched homes looted, known of rapes, descended to the animal in vicious firefights, liberated whole nations from the bootheels of Nazi conquerors and the brutal Japanese, smelled the horror of concentration camps.

Out of that charnel house we had come home alive. Alive! I have no real words for the joy to be alive at that moment in history so long ago: the war was over and we had escaped death. The sky glowed bluer than it ever had before, leaves sheened with the colors of spring and summer, and even cold water became champagne. Women shimmered with a special beauty, their bodies, their warm faces, their breasts, their thighs all a promise and a delight. There was "nothing like a dame." Life, just plain life, was sweet.

And from that life burst hope. The world must change, be purified. The pain and the suffering we had experienced would have its justification in the birth of a new world. I cannot emphasize strongly enough the force of these emotions of hope that swept over us when we returned. And it was not just for me that this hope shone with a special beauty. For a few short months the whole world lived in the belief that people might grow up and that the destruction of humanity and its environment, natural and man-made, would cease. It could not be otherwise. Enemies would become friends. The pain we had experienced and seen would unleash a new social order, a world free of war and built around peace. There would no longer be such disparity in incomes. The poor would be lifted, the weak empowered, the sick given health. People would, at last, after millennia, learn to live together, share their advantages.

The formative convention of the United Nations in April 1945 in San Francisco began the first step toward that new world. This is what my generation had fought for. Our fathers had failed the world by betraying the League of Nations after World War I. Our generation would not be so stupid. Our international organization would work. We had paid for it with blood.

At the University of Chicago, which I attended on Public Law 16, the wounded soldier's version of the G. I. Bill, those hopes for a peaceful and better world motivated many veterans on campus. And we echoed the sentiments of the president of the university, Robert Maynard Hutchins. At the end of the war, he called the atomic bomb "the good news of damnation," believing that the threat of atomic extinction would bring nations together, not drive them to incessant arms races and new kinds of war. Shortly after the bomb fell on Hiroshima and Nagasaki, Hutchins convened an Atomic Energy Control Conference at the university attended by important national figures, including leading politicians and professors.

> Henry Wallace, the secretary of commerce and former vice president [was there, as was] Chairman David Lilienthal of the Tennessee Valley Authority who was soon to head the Atomic Energy Commission. . . . Glenn Seaborg, a future Nobel laureate who worked on the Metallurgy Project in Chicago [which led to the atomic bomb . . . wrote] . . . after the passage of thirty years, "Summoning all the assembled knowledge and reasoning power we could, we had tried to discern some way in which the United States could lead mankind out of its new and seemingly desperate situation. Unencumbered by the details of national bargaining positions, which had not yet emerged, and of the nuclear arms race, which had not yet begun, we were able to raise broad questions that, as the years passed and the political and military landscape became more cluttered, it would prove increasingly difficult to consider."[1]

Out of these deliberations came the Committee to Frame a World Constitution that, two years later, offered the world a proposed constitution to control its warlike tendencies and edge toward a better distribution of the world's resources.[2] Nationwide, the United World Federalists were formed, also seeking that goal of a world government.

Atomic scientists were important proponents

of these efforts. Arthur Compton, a significant leader in the invention of the bomb, wrote, "The years they spent at making atomic bombs prepared those who were making them to burst into a vast missionary call for peace as soon as the war was won. . . . The whole world shall have peace and, as far as the new advances of science and technology can bring it, prosperity and a more complete life. . . . Such is the spirit of the atomic crusade."[3]

The countries of the West, still standing, did not immediately coin the name the "evil empire" for the USSR. Rather, for a moment, there was some hope that the United States, England, and continental Europe could find some *modus vivendi* with Stalin and his minions. After all, they had been our allies in winning the war. In March 1946 the Acheson-Lilienthal report to the United Nations Atomic Energy Commission even suggested a path toward international control of the atomic bomb: "A United Nations atomic energy authority . . . would survey and control all known fissionable ore deposits on earth; license, construct, and monitor all national atomic-energy facilities; and have broad inspection powers to detect any diversion of atomic resources to military purposes."[4] The atomic secret, the monopoly of England and the United States, would be shared for the common good of humanity. National interests would no longer dominate as control shifted to an international agency.

But—and this was a huge codicil—when the report was released to the public, the United States added a statement insisting on its freedom to continue building and testing atomic bombs until the UN atomic energy authority was established. The Soviets insisted in return that the atomic weapon production cease before an international agreement was concluded.[5]

Thus the forty-plus years' arms race between the United States and the USSR began. The United Nations Atomic Energy Committee soon disappeared in an atmosphere of rising nationalism and fear. In the spring of 1946 Stalin said he did not trust the capitalist nations to make peace and Winston Churchill spoke in Fulton, Missouri, of an iron curtain descending over Europe.

The communists and other radical groups, such as the anarchists and the socialists, had been enemies of the establishment in the United States and northern Europe for years. In 1918 the United States and England sent troops to the USSR to try to defeat the "reds." In 1919 America deported those it defined as subversives. In 1919–1920 America put those it deemed communist, anarchist, or socialist in jail. The godless communists wanted to destroy our way of life, went the conventional wisdom, with their opposition to capitalism. At the end of World War II, Gen. George S. Patton, Jr., wanted to take his troops and continue his drive to the east, "taking on" the Russians.[6] The OSS hired former Nazis to be spies on the USSR and its threat to us.[7] By 1946 we feared the USSR would destroy us. It became the face of "Evil" and it had to be contained.

We had discovered a new "enemy" around whom we could organize our national life. In the fall of 1946 a Republican Congress was elected in the United States. The House Un-American Activities Committee became even more virulent in its pursuit of "reds." In the fall of 1947, this committee continued its investigation of Hollywood. Richard Nixon, a member of the committee, was crucial to the conviction of Alger Hiss. Blacklists of movie stars, TV actors, writers, producers, and directors were printed. Men and women in the media were quickly fired even if they were not communists but simply left-leaning, and were sometimes jailed for their opinions.

In that same spring President Truman promulgated the Loyalty Review Board, which investigated existing or potential federal employees for their loyalty to America. States and cities passed anti-subversive legislation. Teachers at public schools and colleges were particularly hounded.[8] The former Nazis hired by the OSS in Europe to give us intelligence about the USSR increased our fear of Stalin and the USSR a hundred-fold. They reported the power of Stalin and his push toward atomic weaponry; they ignored the level of collapse in that nation after the destruction of World War II.[9] We made policy on the first kind of information and ignored the second. Our response was insistence on continued improvement of our atomic weaponry.

In 1949 the USSR exploded its first atomic bomb. In reaction, the United States explored nuclear power in all kinds of tests, culminating in the explosion of the hydrogen bomb in 1952. A poisonous atmosphere seized the land. The "reds" were about to take over. Those of us who had fought in the war and so longed for a peaceful world were betrayed by an all-consuming fear of the "enemy" that bred political repression and destroyed all sense of the hope for a better world born in that brief moment after World War II. Enemies lurked everywhere. Even domestically, one was suspected of being a "red" if supporting social change.

And so often it was a veteran of World War II who led the hunt. The American Legion was in the forefront of the search. The Legion had an Americanism Commission as part of its organization following World War II. The Legion's national commander believed that after the War "a secret battalion of some 75,000 or 80,000 trained Communists and an estimated auxiliary corps of 750,000 to one million dupes, camp followers, secret sympathizers and casual supporters" were active in the United States. He wanted local posts to "organize an unofficial advisory committee" to combat this menace.[10] It got so bad that a legless veteran who had been wounded in 1943 was fired from his job at the Veterans Administration because he was a member of the Socialist Workers Party. "He denied that either he or the SWP [Socialist Workers Party] advocated violent overthrow" of the government.[11]

And, of course, Joe McCarthy, the leader of this attack, was a veteran, elected as a senator from Wisconsin partly because of his nickname, "Tail Gunner Joe." Veterans played a part in the violent riot against the black singer Paul Robeson in September 1949. A politically unpopular veteran was also apt to receive a less than honorable discharge.[12] In Chicago, attempts to integrate veteran's housing were greeted with riots.

For a brief time immediately after the war, a few of us veterans banded together to try and create a different way of thinking about America, the American Veterans Committee. With its motto "citizens first, veterans second," it stood for policies of racial equality, full employment, free speech, and support of the United Nations. But it crashed in the warfare with domestic communists, proven or rumored. A terrible nastiness consumed the land as America discovered another enemy to take the place of the Axis, this enemy not only abroad but within.

Those of us who had come back from the war, determined to make a better world, were attacked as "naïve," "do-gooders," "fellow travelers." It was no longer safe to believe in any form of social change. One instantly was considered a front for communism, branded as one of the "dupes" who supported the communist line. One either signed a loyalty oath as a teacher or an employee of government, or one was fired. It was that simple.

The attack was particularly vicious on anyone who supported racial integration. Taylor Branch in *Pillar of Fire* describes how Martin Luther King, Jr., was harassed for his supposed communist leanings and the supposed communists on his staff.[13] In my personal experience, the head of the Chicago Public Housing Authority, Elizabeth Wood, who wanted to integrate public housing, was fired for her efforts to reach that goal.[14] I knew of the Housing Authority's efforts to integrate veterans housing in Chicago. A friend of mine and fellow ex-student from the University of Chicago, Ed Holmgren, a combat veteran of the Eighth Air Force, responsible for tenant selection in the Housing Authority, was also fired.[15]

Joe McCarthy waved his list of "proven communists" in the State Department. The witch hunt got rid of those consular officers who had worked in China and supposedly helped Mao and his communist army. These American foreign policy experts had "lost China" according to that powerful group of conservatives, "The China Lobby." Blacklists swept radio, movie, newspaper, and magazines clean of left-wingers.

Liberal organizations such as the Americans for Democratic Action denounced communism. The American Civil Liberties Union and the NAACP followed suit.[16] Innocents were destroyed in this process, those never communist but left-leaning, simply interested in equal opportunities for the disenfranchised in the land. I cannot overemphasize the fear that gripped people of good intent in those long-ago times, how wide the net was thrown to intimidate and frighten all liberal opinion. Some liberals, in their fear, either shut up, joined the witch hunt, or masked their beliefs.

In those long years from 1946 to 1956 or so, the "old left" in America was destroyed, not only by arrest and intimidation, but also by the cowardice of many who masked their sympathies. The consequence? When the new left came into being in the 1960s, it never had a firm base rooted in the past; the long tradition of social concern that stretched back into the eighteenth century was lost.[17] The left has really never recovered from that impact, weakened by the destruction of its deep roots in the American national character. The left also disappeared because people were intimidated. They shut up, signed loyalty oaths, trimmed their jibs, and rode out the storms of the day in the safest havens to be found.

The bitter denunciation of suspected communist party members and its followers ended all hope of a "brave, new world," the one we longed for after the Allied victory. The dream of a world government and international control of the atomic bomb disappeared in an ever-increasing arms race and defense build-up that still haunts us. The intensity of the repression of those with unpopular opinions for those few years can scarcely be understood today. Though comparison is made with the repression under the Patriot Act, there is as yet none of the hysteria that swept across the land after 1946 when, essentially, all liberal opinions became suspect.

These were the moments when the veterans of World War II might have really shown they belonged to the "Greatest Generation" by opposing the political repression and hysteria that so darkened the land. But only a few of us so acted. Most shut up as the fear of our newest enemy spread. World government, the hope for international control of atomic power, disappeared in increasing competition and warfare among nation-states. Nations now live in constant fear of each other, fear of each other's atomic weaponry, fear of other nation-states with their panoply of arms, fear that they will become atomic powers, fear of the terrorist willing to die in a suicide attack.

The hope that the United Nations would make a difference disappeared as the world split into two bitter camps, communist and capitalist.

This radical shift in policy in the United States was perhaps best epitomized by the transition of one man, Cord Meyer, Jr., from internationalist to Cold War warrior. Wounded in the head as a Marine lieutenant in the South Pacific, he almost lost his sight, then wrote a famous and wonderful short story of that event which was published in the *Atlantic Monthly*. He became one of the advisors to the birth of the United Nations and helped form the American Veterans Committee. As president of the United World Federalists, he supported world government. But then, as the competition between the Western allies—the United States, Britain, France, West Germany—and the USSR became nastier, he turned from a believer in world government and international control of the atomic secret to a committed warrior against the Soviet Union. He helped reject any member of the communist party in the American Veterans Committee, a struggle that so alienated veterans such as myself that we simply quit. Later he devoted his career to working for the CIA.[18]

As more Third World nations were added to the United Nations and its membership began to reflect a harsh anti-Americanism, the result of communist influence over the world, votes in the General Assembly increasingly condemned the United States. America slowly changed from a supporter of the UN to a bitter critic of its practices, and in later years even refused to pay its allotted percentage of the UN budget. The hope that the United Nations might bring about a more peaceful world, the hope of the powerless and wounded peoples of so many nations after World War II, was forgotten; the belief that nations and individuals could together form a more peaceful union virtually disappeared in the United States. Emphasis centered on our battle with the USSR and how to win it, no matter whom we supported or joined in the gutter, no matter what regimes we overthrew.

That moment just after World War II when peace seemed possible is no longer reported, not even remembered. Our hopes for a peaceful world were quickly killed by the rise of the Cold War.

~∾~

After we returned from the war, a bunch of us who had been in combat rented a house together while we attended the University of Chicago. One of us mentioned the war one evening after dinner. Another quipped about an article or book he had read—he thought it was by Bill Mauldin—that described a proper memorial to the war: every town should dig a hole four feet deep and ten feet wide in the town square, fill it with excrement, and let it rot. That summarized the opinion of some of us about the war.

Our sense of the appalling nature of the war drove us to struggle for world peace, to seek Roosevelt and Churchill's Four Freedoms, the goals of World War II, so forgotten today: freedom of speech and expression, freedom of worship, freedom from want, freedom from fear. But we watched our longing for world peace slowly dwindle as the nation plunged into the Cold War, an arms race between ourselves and the USSR the common denominator between two world powers. When McCarthyism reared its ugly head, we saw it gobble up those we had respected. We even feared for ourselves.

The hopes for peace we had brought from the war crashed about our heads. War and preparation for it became the common theme of America.

~⮿~

Among those in uniform during World War II, the few of us who had actually been in combat and who understood the awful consequences of the force we had applied to win World War II always remained a minority. At the most it is estimated that only eight hundred thousand men really saw hard combat in Europe,[19] less in the South Pacific, perhaps, at the most, a total of a million and a half soldiers, sailors, and marines, maybe ten percent of all those in service. Compared to Europe, the USSR, and Japan, the vast majority of Americans experienced few traumatic consequences of the war. In fact, Americans lived in a wonderfully protected world, except for those whose sons, fathers, husbands, and other family members were wounded or killed.

And, in retrospect, few combat veterans from Europe or the South Pacific took the stance we did at the university, of being politically active for peace. We came home to a nation that had seen none of the acts of atrocity we had seen and that could not even imagine that they had occurred. In terms of violence and war, the media proved itself incapable of presenting the real horror that went with personal experience of combat. So most of us eventually shut up about what we had seen. We were never given the opportunity to grieve for all we had lived through:

friends with bellies ripped open, towns destroyed, civilians lying in pornographic postures of death at the edge of villages we liberated, women raped. We repressed our memories. Even more we repressed what we had done.

The movies, the media slowly captured the telling of our story, leading to the recent books of the Ambroses and the Brokaws. War became a time of courage and comradeship, far from the realities through which we had lived. We did not challenge such interpretations. We took a few years to recover—bummed around, maybe drank too much, slept around—but then the nation plunged into the most fantastic orgy of consumerism ever known.

We forgot all we had seen and learned in combat. As we aged and reached retirement, media stars and politicians made us into heroes again: the men who had beaten the Great Depression and won World War II. We had forgotten that out of both the pain and the triumph of that great victory in 1945, a momentary bridge over the fear of "enemies" among nations had been built, a trust that, to be maintained, required patient attention and careful nurturing, efforts that the United States, under the leadership of my generation, refused, fearful of giving away any of our sovereignty in a Cold War. We helped form and, then, accepted those Myths of World War II. The cooperative agreements that might have been established to reach a peaceful world completely disappeared over sixty years of interminable warfare. Fear of unknown and all-powerful "enemies"—Koreans, Vietnamese, Muslims—has taken their place, enemies that can only be met by threats and acts of great armies committed to war.

And, so, my "Greatest Generation" of Americans failed in its responsibility to lead our country and the world toward a place of mutual trust as we stood all-powerful in our victory. We failed in the search for peace. Though we helped our Allies and bound the wounds of the defeated, we sank into a forty-year confrontation that broke into haunted warfare in Korea and Vietnam and in smaller nations over the globe.

Our legacy now is but another monument of marble and granite on the Mall in Washington, the same cold stone plinths and platitudes as those rewarded to veterans of the Revolution and the Civil War. How I wish that my generation's gift to the future might have been one of peace instead of these countless, cruel wars and battles and bombings that have left around four hundred thousand of our young men and women killed or wounded, many hostage to Post Traumatic Stress Disorder, with millions of innocent civilians, so many women and children, killed in countless Third World nations. Oh, how I wish that we had led the United States to an international control of the atomic bomb instead of this incessant and virulent arms race that so frightens us today. How I wish we had led the United States into the wisdom of limiting our sovereignty by leading the nations of the earth toward a world government, instead of our ruthless dedication to power, empire, and almost continuous war so as to maintain our arrogance and our hegemony.

How much safer the world would be today if we had so acted. We failed our higher responsibility. If we had performed greater acts of peace, leading the world away from its incessant commitment to war and weaponry, then, truly, we might deserve to be named the "Greatest Generation."

The simple truth is that we are a terribly failed generation. Certainly, we won the war and our fathers and mothers beat the Great Depression. Certainly we did all those things of which Steven Ambrose and Tom Brokaw so movingly speak. But in doing them we lost part of our soul. The accumulation of things became more important than the creation of real opportunity for men and women of all colors and classes. The fear of enemies became more important than trust among strangers. The importance of power became more important than the compassion for the poor, the weak, the sick, and the lonely. The killing of innocents became routine, "collateral damage."

The movies, the books, the memoirs, the stories that tell our children of our courage and our strength apply to us only in our youth. For that moment, some of us may truly have been heroes. For that moment, some of us may have reached out far beyond ourselves.

Perhaps, now, as we age, near death, we can at last perform one more service for this country we love and for which many died. Perhaps now, at last, we can tell the truth about who we are and what we have become, our last act of service to this nation we so love.

Part III

The Third Myth: "We Won World War II Largely on Our Own"

CHAPTER 8

America Triumphant

P erhaps the oddest of the myths of World War II is the belief in the popular mind that the United States won that war by ourselves. For years I have scanned newspapers, listened to public radio, watched regular and public television, watched movies, and read books (novels, memoirs, and non-fiction) about that war, and seldom in mainstream media and literature is the contribution of other nations given full credit in our victory over Germany, Japan, and Italy.

Credit still goes largely to us, as so clearly shown in President George W. Bush's trip to Europe for the celebration of the sixtieth anniversary of the defeat of Germany. Instead of thanking the Russians for the enormous contribution made in the victory over the Nazis, he chastised that nation for their actions at the end of the war in taking over Eastern Europe.[1] Another important opportunity was lost in which we could have led the world and its many leaders toward a better understanding of what the word "allied" meant in World War II. Even our movies—such as *Stalingrad*—portray the soldiers of the USSR as "Evil," killing their own troops, and do not cite that country's enormous sacrifices and contributions to victory as a beleaguered nation. We forget that in the battle of Stalingrad in the winter of 1942–1943 and the surrender there of General Paulus's Sixth German Army to the USSR, and in the battle of Kursk in July 1943, the greatest tank battle of all times, the back of the German army was broken.[2] In his book about D-Day, Stephen Ambrose actually has the audacity to subtitle it *The Climactic Battle of World War II*. He neatly forgets that if German troops had not been pinned down by the USSR on D-Day and substantially defeated in these earlier battles, there is little chance the Allied landing would have succeeded. And, while the role of the USSR is largely neglected with its eleven to thirteen million military deaths, the enormous contribution of China in defeating Japan, "tying up almost a million Japanese troops that might have been used against MacArthur and Nimitz" according to John Toland, is practically ignored.[3]

The exception to the belief in our own triumphalism, of course, lies in our recognition of the role of Great Britain. The bombings of England before we entered the war and the voice of Churchill are particularly remembered. After that we sometimes hear vague references to Market Garden and the British invasion on the beaches of Juno, Sword, and Gold on D-Day, but there is little sense that the Commonwealth casualties in the war were greater than ours, that Britain held the fort for years before Pearl Harbor.

Three aspects of American culture help explain our certainty in this myth that we largely won the war on our own. The first is our history of warfare from the founding of our nation, rooted in a tradition of victory in war for over three hundred years from colonial times to D-Day. The second is the combative individualism, the will to win, which has helped to define American character. The third rises from our enormous capacity to produce armaments that both let us serve as the arsenal of democracy in World War II and forms the base for our place today as the most mighty military power of all time.

~◈~

Our constant experience of war from the settlement of the nation until today is so deeply buried in the American unconscious that we scarcely recognize it. As a nation we have always triumphed in our many wars, largely without allies or, when we have had them, we were the first among those allies. The particular quality of this experience of war has helped make the American national character what it is. As Page Smith writes in *A New Age Now Begins*:

> Between 1700 and 1763 the colonists had been involved in five "intercolonial" wars, culminating in the dramatic struggle with the French for Canada. There can be no doubt that these wars, taxing as they were to colonial resources, did serve in a notable way to draw the colonies closer together—or to prevent them from flying apart, split a dozen ways by petty feuds and jealousies. The wars were, in short, an essential training ground, a primary element in the slowly emerging consciousness of Americans. Like their common grievances against the mother country, their common French enemy was a compelling force for unity.[4]

To the reality of these colonial wars, rooted in struggles in Europe, must be added the constant and

terrifying wars fought against Native Americans during and before the eighteenth century, beginning
with the Pequot War in 1637. Wars with Native
Americans continued in 1675 with King Philip's War
in New England and of course there were bitter frontier struggles in the other colonies as well. Then
came the crushing expulsion of the five "civilized
tribes" from the South in the 1830s, ending with the
bitter warfare west of the Mississippi River after the
Civil War and the final defeat of all Native American
nations by the 1890s.[5] Earlier, from 1812 to 1815,
we fought our final war with England; then in 1846–
1848, we invaded Mexico, and after that came the
cruel and nation-defining war between the North and
South from 1861 to 1865 over the Union and slavery. We had another war of conquest against Spain
in 1898 that led to the possession of outposts in the
Caribbean and the Pacific, requiring us to crush the
Philippine insurrectionists, followed by our incur-
sion into Mexico in 1916. In 1917 we ignored George
Washington's warning about foreign entanglements
and returned to Europe as a combatant. In 1941 we
followed suit. From 1950 until today we have been
engaged in three major wars in Third World countries and in many smaller conflagrations, as well as
indirect efforts at influencing and changing the governments of nations from Central and South America
to the Middle and Far East.[6]

War as much as any other experience has
helped make us into a nation.

And much of that warlike ability and capacity
has come from conducting and winning our wars
largely by ourselves. In World War I we insisted on
using American troops in our army alone, not as part
of other national forces (except for the all African
American 369th Regiment that fought under the
French). In World War II, of course, we were not

alone, yet we fought that way in the Pacific. Even in Europe, the American army was seldom under other commands—and when it was, as in the drop at Arnhem in Operation Market Garden in the fall of 1944, the experiment seldom worked. Further, the American media presented World War II from our perspective, and an American general, Dwight D. Eisenhower, was the Supreme Commander of the European Allied Forces. We believe American troops and American matériel defeated the Germans, Japanese, and Italians, culminating in the explosion of the atomic bombs. Though we may have had allies, in much of the popular mind, America was largely responsible for the winning of that war, its allies fighting in lesser roles. And, after the Cold War began, of course, any contribution of the USSR as an ally in World War II was repressed. It became the newest "enemy," so how could it ever have helped us win a war?

Though we did cooperate with other countries that formed the North Atlantic Treaty Organization in the Cold War, aided us in our wars in Korea and Vietnam, forged an alliance with us in the Gulf War, and made limited partnerships with us in the war in Iraq, in all these efforts we have remained "top dog," stated or unstated. We protect our sovereignty.

Deep within us, so deep we scarcely acknowledge it, even understand it, resonates this memory of triumph in wars we largely fought alone. It is a tradition that creates within us a driving will to win over all enemies. In World War II, it helped us rebound from the surprise attack at Pearl Harbor and the subsequent loss of the South Pacific territories to a grim and determined will to victory.[7]

~∾~

If fighting and winning a war largely by ourselves is part of the American national character, another aspect of that character throughout our history that helps explain our need to go it alone is our combative individualism. As a people we have rewarded individual behavior over corporate effort except for a few moments in our history. This faith in individualism is a breeding ground for the myth of the violent and lone American male who takes on the forces of "Evil" by himself and destroys them, triumphant over his and his community's enemies. This chord resonates greatly with our past. Deep within us lies that memory: the Leatherstocking of James Fenimore Cooper,[8] the cowboy of Gary Cooper in *High Noon* and Allen Ladd in *Shane*, and of John Wayne in countless movies, Clint Eastwood as *Dirty Harry,* the detectives of Dashiell Hammett, Rick of *Casablanca,* even Luke Skywalker of *Star Wars*— all share similar characteristics. They are men who ride into town alone, destroy the "Evil" enemy, and ride off into the sunset alone, never able to establish a family or community for themselves, always cursed by a memory of violence done by them or to them and to those they love. In this myth it is impossible for the American to have long-term allies or long-term commitments. For a moment this American hero may function as a member of society, have friends, even a family, but then he leaves, riding on his lonely way. Is it too far a stretch to see our international relations in this way? I think not. We are uncomfortable with too many permanent allies. We work best alone. America does not easily cooperate with others unless we are the central character.[9]

~≈~

And yet, in World War II America's role as the producer of the cornucopia of armaments for the Allies from China and the USSR to England was, perhaps, its most important contribution to winning the war. Here this myth of winning the war alone holds an essential truth about Allied victory in World War II. For example, in 1939 we produced 5,856 airplanes; in 1944, 85,998. In 1941 we built 544 ocean-going vessels; in 1944, 2,654. The same astounding growth in production occurred with all kinds of military equipment, from tanks to rifles to artillery pieces.[10] These industrial efforts were no less than miracles. Without such an astounding contribution of military matériel the Axis would never have been defeated. Our world would be different today.

Our ability to produce such plentitude of military goods in so short a time, combined with our history of victory in war, our will to win, and our aggressive individualism, help convince us that we won World War II largely on our own. Our problem today is that, in so believing, we neglect the burden our allies carried in winning that war, the enormous pain that other nations suffered. Though we provided the goods for winning the war and a vast armed force for fighting it, they—particularly the USSR and China—carried a far greater burden than we did.

Approximately 292,000 American troops were killed in combat in World War II, with over 670,000 wounded. For my generation and that of my parents, these numbers were appalling. We knew the suffering of our loved ones; we knew the loss of a generation of men who deserved their lives and happiness and who might have made great contributions to the nation.

We still do not understand that this burden of pain was far greater for our allies. The British Commonwealth suffered 344,000 combat deaths. The

USSR lost somewhere between eleven million and thirteen million soldiers in its armies alone. China's numbers seem almost impossible to determine: estimates of military deaths range from two and a half million to as high as eleven million. We do know that France had two hundred thousand men killed in action. (And our enemies experienced far greater losses than we did: Germany, Japan, and Italy together lost six to eight million men in combat).[11]

In terms of time, the burden of fighting was just as unequal. The United States was in the war for around three years and nine months, Britain, France, and our other European allies almost six years, and the USSR over four years, while China and its enemy Japan fought each other for fourteen long years. Germany experienced almost six years of war, Italy a little over five.

Civilian casualties were even more favorable to the United States. Once again, the USSR's figures far exceeded those of any other nation with losses in the vicinity of twenty million, and perhaps, according to the newest studies, as many as forty million. Poland lost six million, half of them Jews—twenty percent of its population. Again, China's figures are difficult to discern, but some estimates are as high as twenty million between civil war and war with Japan. France had four hundred thousand men, women, and children killed; one hundred and ninety thousand Dutch citizens were killed; sixty thousand British civilians died, largely from the bombing raids.[12]

Losses to infrastructure and cultural monuments were just as disproportionate. French cities, particularly in Normandy, were dismantled by both airplane bombing and artillery fire. Britain lost many of its architectural treasures. The disaster to the environment in the USSR from the Ukraine to Leningrad was inconceivable, with not just cities and towns but whole landscapes ravaged by fire and depredation.

Destruction of the enemy's environment was at least as severe. Whole cities in Germany from Hamburg to Dresden nearly disappeared. Japan's major cities, from Tokyo to Hiroshima and Nagasaki, were almost obliterated.

The mainland of America knew none of this ruin. Civilians experienced the war second-hand through its media that, understandably, concentrated on the contribution of the nation and its troops, unable to give a real sense of the unforgiving wasteland in Europe, the USSR, and Japan. Because of our production of matériel, our economy grew at an incredible rate. Though Americans were constrained by rationing, it was far less severe than that for other Allied nations. For most Americans, war did become a "Good," and they also believed that we won the war largely on our own. America's role as the arsenal of democracy saw to that. Americans seldom made and saved as much money, a source of the explosive economic growth after the war.

~⟨~⟩~

Consequently, this myth is perhaps the most complex of all as it contains a fundamental truth: without America's economic might, there would have been no victory. Yet, what mythmakers worship is not just this enormous contribution to the Allied effort, but the glory and heroism of frontline firefights, rooted in our memories of victory and our combative individualism, and ever-present in movies, TV spectaculars, and video games. In so doing mythmakers neglect the burden other nations carried as well as their role in military victory.

Believing that we won World War II largely on our own leads us to the certainty that we can "go it alone" in our foreign relations. We don't need anybody. We can do it on our own. We denigrate the United Nations, even appoint delegates who loathe the concept of internationalism. For almost sixty years we have dedicated ourselves to this faith in our own supremacy. Our weapons are the best. Our army is the largest. We need no one. We fear no one. Our policies of preemption and military dominance, the Bush administration's stands, show that faith in our own power to wage and win war by ourselves anywhere on the globe is never questioned. President Bush expressed this most forcefully when, after 9/11, he was heard to say, "I don't care what the international lawyers say, we are going to kick some ass."[13]

In so leading the nation into war, the president missed a marvelous opportunity. For a moment, much of the world had been joined with America in sympathy and support for those who had been killed and injured in the terrorist attacks on the World Trade Center and Pentagon. He had the opportunity to lead those nations into new peaceful and cooperative ways of fighting terrorism. Instead we did "kick ass," first in Afghanistan and then in Iraq—and years later are still bogged down in those countries with, as yet, no clear exit and with casualty lists inexorably rising.

A central attribute of going it alone is the buildup of the most mighty military force in history. Once we had it we felt honor-bound to use it. We see the use of that military—war—as the central means to deal with terrorism. Other nations insist on law enforcement. We insist on war, furthering our isolation. Other nations search for other causes for terrorism and a more peaceful way to defuse terrorism. We insist on violence.

The lives of innocents and our soldiers should not be held in thrall to such a primitive and rash certainty that war is always the best solution to our international problems. We are certain that, if necessary, we can wage war alone—the international community be damned—and that we will always win, given our crushing might. The consequences of such arrogance are now obvious in Iraq and in the promise of wars without end. These wars, waged alone, impose human, financial, and material costs borne both by us and, as always, by our troops and the innocent civilians of those nations we define as the enemy, their environment and their infrastructure ravaged while once again our people and our land remain untouched.

Is this the America of which we can be proud? Is this the America that *helped* win World War II? In this new century, it is no longer possible to go alone.

Part IV

The Fourth Myth:
"When Evil Lies in Others, War Is the Means to Justice"

CHAPTER 9

The Holocaust and the "Evil" Other

Perhaps the most powerful of our memories of World War II is the Holocaust, the murder of six million Jews and of six million other "undesirables" by all those barbaric methods of killing innocents on the ground described earlier. These memories are inextricably linked to the image of American troops liberating the concentration camps. Over the years those two recollections of World War II have fused and produced one important lesson: there is a great potential for evil in the human being and only war can bring justice. Cooperation equals appeasement and both have become dirty words, the work of cowards or, worse, sniveling collaborators.

These memories of "Good" overcoming "Evil" are used today to simplify and justify entry into new wars. They raise fierce emotions of purity. Our mighty arms will triumph. The president and his administration used these arguments to the fullest extent in stirring up American feelings against Saddam Hussein, who became equated with Hitler. Whenever I talk with people, strangers, even friends, and I ask if war is the answer to a current repressive regime, the argument—what about Hitler and the

Holocaust?—is immediately raised: "You can't appease a dictator."

Hitler and the Holocaust were human disasters of the worst kind, and war, the force of arms, was the only way to stop what was clearly one of the most despicable events in human history. Yet, over the years, I have slowly—and agonizingly, I must admit—learned to question this argument about the dangers of cooperation and appeasement in our newer wars. I now wonder if it is not time to turn to different and better ways than war to react to those we define as "Evil." This learning has demanded unraveling an established thought pattern of many years, allowing me to reach conclusions far different than the certainty that evil always lies in others and war is the means to justice. This tortuous path of learning involved both a long and difficult personal journey and a twenty-five year exploration of American and European history.

~✑~

The personal journey began with my awareness of atrocity. I first became aware that I lived in an age of industrial warfare in the 1930s as a young boy when I saw the photograph of a baby, crying, left alone, clothes torn, bloodied, sitting on the pavement in Shanghai after a bombing or the explosion of an artillery shell.[1] For over sixty years that image has seared my mind, teaching me the meaning of atrocity: an innocent suffering pain and death inflicted by a force far greater than him/herself, a force of implacable destruction to which the life beneath it is meaningless. This force differs from a natural disaster—hurricane, tornado, flood—in that it has a human will behind it.

We name that force and the people who use it "Evil."

My childhood was formed by such images and threats of such atrocities—the Japanese invasion of China in 1931; the Italian conquest of Abyssinia (Ethiopia) in 1935; the Spanish Civil War from 1936 to 1939; the bombing of the USS *Panay* and the rape of Nanking in 1937; the constant rumblings of the Nazis in Europe, from their seizure of power in 1933 to the burning of books, the first concentration camps in 1933, the bombing of Guernica in Spain in 1937, the *Kristallnacht* of 1938; and the many invasions of smaller nations, all for the policy of "living space" for Germany.[2]

I learned early that atrocities came from other nations, never from ourselves. The United States was free of such barbarities. The lynchings of African Americans, for example, were never reported in the papers I read or news reports I heard.

Yet, in those long-ago years before World War II, when I was in my early teens, there was another inheritance that touched my conscience, one scarcely recognized or remembered today. Still so close to the horror of trench warfare of World War I, Americans were not so certain then that war was the means to justice, to stop atrocity, to halt the "Evil" we read of in newspapers. Throughout our past, doubts about war existed in all parts of the political spectrum. On the political right there was the America First Movement, dedicated to the proposition that "foreign entanglements" were un-American and dangerous to the republic. On the left there was a strong pacifist sentiment, rising from the memory of the terrible slaughter from 1914 to 1918 and dedicated to the belief that war was morally wrong. Opposition to war expressed itself in a variety of ways, from parades and marches to such movies as *All Quiet on the Western Front* and such books as *Johnny Got His Gun.*

The attack on Pearl Harbor instantly changed those beliefs. We were now in a life-and-death struggle with the makers of atrocity. We once again were certain that the "Evil" in the world could only be reduced by war.

A year before I entered the army, in the winter of 1941–1942, my mother belonged to the Book-of-the-Month Club. One of the books she received was *Out of the Night* by Jan Valtin, its title taken from the poem by William Ernest Henley. I have heard, over a lifetime, so many fervently say that America did not know of the Holocaust in Germany until after the concentration camps were discovered in 1944 by the USSR and in 1945 by the Allied Forces. But here was a book that I read in my safe bedroom in a western suburb of Chicago in 1942 when I was seventeen. It told a story of the concentration camps in 1935 and 1936 that simply blew apart my young mind.

I must quote a little of what I read then, for these few descriptions from *Out of the Night* told me more of the world in which I would live than any other lesson I received in a loving middle-class home when I was a boy.

> On the stretcher lay the mangled corpse of the Jew who had been murdered at night. His abdomen was a smear of dried blood and a clump of bloody rubbish was where his genitals had been. His face was convulsed and his eyes, wide open, were twisted upwards in a glassy stare. The guard in the doctor's garb led the stretcher crew past the lined-up prisoners, and all of us stared silently at the dead man. The corpse was naked and the gulls cruised close and screamed. . . . At a

command, the stretcher-bearers dumped their burden on the ground close to the rim of the hole.

Several of the Jews who were standing around the hole clasped their hands in front of their faces. Two others collapsed. They were cuffed and beaten until they stood straight again.

"Pants down," commanded Toussaint.

The row of Jews lowered their pants. They were not men anymore. They were animals without a will. They were stiff with fear.

"Now masturbate," commanded Toussaint.

A few of the Jews reached for their genitals. Guards ran along their file and struck the others in their faces.

"Masturbate, I said," Toussaint roared. "Masturbate, you swine."

The Jews obeyed. They feebly went through the motions that were demanded of them and many of the guards wore broad grins.

"Faster," Toussaint shouted. "You desert bandits! You lustful reptiles! Show us how you do it in your cells at night."

The Jews pretended to masturbate faster. They knew they would be beaten if they did not. They knew they could not afford to collapse.[3]

No one knew if the Allies would be victorious in the winter of 1941–42. But the whole Western world did know more about the atrocities of war than many now admit. That knowledge, I am certain, was a factor that led me to volunteer for the army and, then, for line duty out of a safe college billet.

In France in that summer of 1944 I saw first hand the atrocities of total, industrial war: the bombed out towns of Normandy; civilians fleeing along highways; slave laborers who had worked for a long four years in the iron and coal mines of Lorraine; my platoon was even carefully examined by a woman who had been raped by an American soldier. We stood in formation at attention while she walked slowly between our lines and painfully scrutinized our faces. I did not even know what rape was then, I was so young and innocent. Only many years later did I begin to understand the meaning of this rape line-up when a friend of mine who had served with the Fourth Division told me that his war experience had been spent watching a few American soldiers rape and loot their way across Europe.

Later that summer I experienced the liberation of those slave workers, saw both the wonders that freedom bought and, simultaneously, the anger against the scapegoat. It was the glory of liberation that I remembered, the fact that these people had been treated so abominably and that our arms had freed them; it was the pain of the scapegoat I forgot.

Seriously wounded the next day, I was back in the United States by the spring of 1945, appalled by the newsreels showing liberated concentration camps, starved bodies, glassy eyes, piles of discarded corpses. Instantly I knew the scenes were true reflections of the pitiless reality I had already experienced. I then had full faith in the political hope of the Jewish people for a nation, and applauded when President Truman recognized Israel. I believed wholeheartedly in this fourth myth that had evolved from World War II.

~~~

Over the years following our victory in World War II, I watched our faith in the goodness of our arms in crushing the dark enemy slowly evolve into a certain kind of mindset that has come to dominate American thought. I call it "apocalyptic thinking"—the "Evil" in the world will be eradicated by the forces of "Good" that America represents. When President Bush and his administration brand terrorists as "Evil," when President Bush and his administration say "you are with us or against us," when they create the weaponry of "shock and awe," they arm themselves with a black-and-white way of seeing reality that rises directly from World War II and the defeat of the Nazis and their Holocaust.

This apocalyptic thinking dominates not only the administration but, as noted in the presidential elections of 2004, a majority of voting Americans as well, who supported the war in Iraq by voting for President Bush. The terrorist "enemy" we fear, the enemy we must destroy, is "Evil," performing monstrous acts that deny all humanity, all decency, all compassion. Terrorists represent the dark forces of the mind, the howl of madness. Crushing them performs the work of God. Since "Evil" exists outside ourselves, never within, in other nations and people across the world, violence and war are not only necessary, they become "Good," the only means to free and to protect innocents from barbaric forces beyond control. We can do with our enemies as we please, jail them, hold them without trial as long as we like. We can torture them in the same way the Nazis tortured Jews in the concentration camp of Dachau.[4] Apocalyptic thinking leads easily to the dehumanization of our Muslim prisoners. After all they have committed sins and know of other sins soon to occur. We have the right to use them as we please, since they are sub-human in all ways.

America is destined by God to stand tall over the world, pure, undefiled.

This thinking is exacerbated by the religious fundamentalism so prevalent in the world today. There are Christians, Jews, and Muslims who possess this trait of dividing the world into "Good" and "Evil." Each of these religions has its conservative sects and each of these sects sees the others as specters from hell. Jews fear Muslims. Muslims fear Jews. Christians fear Muslims. Muslims fear Christians. Each commits atrocity upon the other. Each is unable to forgive the other. Some American fundamentalists even long for the Holy Land to be fully occupied by Jews so Christ can return and the "rapture" occur.

We have watched the state of Israel dehumanize the citizens of Palestine and demonize its leaders. We have watched the suicide bombers of Palestine retaliate against Israelis. In both cases it is innocents who suffer the most. Bin Laden calls on his followers to kill all Americans. Abu Musab al-Zarqawi follows suit. Israeli settlers in Palestine slaughter Palestinians. Palestinians kill Israelis, women and children, as an inhuman species meant only for destruction.

Since the concentration camps were liberated by American, British, and Russian forces at the end of World War II, the ability to see shades of gray has almost disappeared from the popular mind and particularly from the media. Think on what we saw in 1945: the starved bodies of Jews and other "undesirables" in the concentration camps, scarcely alive, skin and bones, dead bodies lying in obscene postures close to them, and we scarcely knew who was alive, who was dead. Bill Montgomery, the lifelong friend of mine who helped liberate Dachau, says he knows there is "Evil" in the world: he smelled it.

Remember all the other images of innocents killed and maimed we have seen through these years from Vietnam to Bosnia? Are not the perpetrators of such acts "Evil"? Is not striking them down the work of a just God and a just nation?

Such certainty about our ability to judge others has become part of who we are as a nation for the last sixty years. During the Cold War, the Russians took on the mantle of the "enemy," as did the North Koreans, the Chinese, the Vietcong, and all the others we have fought. Now the terrorist is equated with the SS Trooper or the guard at a communist Gulag in our minds, an evil and super-human force destroying innocents. The terrorists, al Qaeda, bin Laden, Saddam Hussein, now Abu Musab al-Zarqawi, become the symbols of that enemy. We have formed a mighty armada, the mightiest of all time, to "defend" ourselves against the newest "enemy" of the day.

We must always have the greatest armed forces, the best weapons technology, no matter the cost. There never has been a downside to these beliefs or their moral certainty. The lessons of World War II have been so clear: there are bad people in the world and arms are necessary to defeat them and protect the innocent. Smash 'em! Kill 'em! Arm for the next enemy who is certain to rise. Somewhere out there are the "Evil" ones lurking in the darkness. Out of our purity and our strength we must defeat them.

~~~

For years I shared these beliefs, confirmed by my own experience in the liberation of France from the Nazis. But I slowly learned that this fourth Myth of World War II, our refusal to ever consider compromise with others we define as "enemies" and our dependence on our force of arms to defeat them, was rooted in America's refusal to understand history, our own and that of the rest of the world.

By concentrating exclusively on the Holocaust as the central event of World War II, seeing the atrocities committed there by another nation, Germany, seeing ourselves as the white knight that stopped the torture of the concentration camps, we have assiduously avoided our own sins of ethnic cleansing. We have never looked as carefully at our propensities for violence, the hatred we bear the stranger, the dark-skinned minority, as we have at the actions of the Germans toward the Jews. Only now, centuries after the fact, are museums in Washington opening to show our destruction of Native Americans and African Americans. Only now do we begin to see replicas of slave markets, slave cabins, and the lynching tree. Only now do we honor the memory of all the Native American cultures before the arrival of Columbus, cultures now destroyed. We have yet to conduct studies and publish books that deal with the psychological make-up of U.S. soldiers who perpetuated the destruction of Native Americans. We have yet to acknowledge the sort of person who profited from slavery for so many generations, or understand the character of the people who formed lynch mobs.

I discovered facts about America's past I really did not want to know. I came to understand how intimate war and atrocities were to our history. I read, for example, about the Pequot War of 1637 of which Cotton Mather wrote, "No less that 600 Pequot souls were brought down to hell that day."[5] I read about our countless wars against Native Americans, leading to their brutal suppression as we took their land; the enraged bitterness of the Civil War; the killings and depredations on the borders in Missouri and

Kansas; the murder of black soldiers at Fort Pillow; the water tortures applied to helpless prisoners in the Philippines in the early part of the twentieth century.

I read of William Calley and the atrocities he and his men committed at My Lai in Vietnam in 1968. Now, in 2004, I saw the newest photographs of the torture and humiliation of Iraqi prisoners by U.S. soldiers in that war-torn country and read the reports of some of our soldiers abusing Iraqi citizens on the street. These photographs were but a vulgar repetition of the book I had read by Jan Valtin in 1942. We now humiliated our prisoners with masturbation just as the SS had humiliated the Jews.

The Defense Department and generals of the army had purposely and cynically violated the Geneva Conventions for the protection of prisoners because of policy statements issued by the president's solicitor, now the attorney general. The coarsening I had observed in society after World War II, making it easier for the combat infantryman to kill, had been at work in Iraq as well, depersonalizing the Muslim into a creature fit only for cruel punishment.

In 1993 Bill Montgomery, Bob Reed, and I visited the concentration camp at Dachau. In the museum I saw a photograph that appalled me: two prisoners with their wrists in handcuffs behind their backs. Their chained wrists had then been raised above their shoulders and locked to a tree trunk above their heads. All their weight hung on their wrists and shoulders, their chests so contorted they could not breathe, a form of crucifixion. A third prisoner, dead, slumped on the ground before them. A Nazi guard stared with disdain at the dead man.[6] In 2005 I read an article in the *New Yorker* about a Muslim prisoner, Manadel al-Jamadi, who was tortured to death in the same way at Abu Ghraib under the control of the CIA.[7]

I watched again and again and again the movie, *Open City*, about the control of Rome by the Nazis in 1943–44. What appalled me most was how the torture of the members of the Italian Resistance by the Gestapo of the German Occupation involved women, women as betrayers or women as facilitators of the abuse. The movie reminded me of the photographs of the sexual humiliation of Muslim prisoners by our female guards. The *New York Times* told of the continual use of female military officers in the interrogation of the prisoners.[8]

What had we become? What did this mean? For Christ's sake, what did all this mean? Had we become the enemy, the "Evil" now lying within us? Who were we? I asked. America was a land I loved, a land I had almost been killed for . . . yet here was the evidence of a different nation than the one I so adored. How could I deal with this reality?

My belief that "Evil" always lay in others as the way to understand the events of today slowly crumbled. There had been terrible acts committed in World War II, acts of such inhumanity they could never be understood. I had seen them. Bad people, men and women, did those things. They had to be stopped. But—and it was a huge "but" on which I stumbled—we, the America I loved, had committed our own acts of barbarity, from the suppression of Native Americans to the enslaving and lynching of African Americans to our continued neglect of the poor and the weak and the mad. Some of these acts equaled the barbarism of the Nazis—not all, of course, but some, especially the fact that we had once owned slaves and, in contrast to most other nations in the world, did not give them up without a war. Were we always so right when we applied the idea of the "Holocaust" to the acts of others, when we claimed so easily the other was "Evil" and we were "Good," leaving no room for compromise? Treating the "enemy" of the day, from the Vietnamese to Muslims, with contempt, disdain, and dehumanization, the way the Nazis treated the Jews, seemed to have become a fixed part of the American national character. We were as guilty of these contemptible acts as the citizens of any other nation. Each time we go to war this hidden part of the American soul bursts to the surface and, once activated, kills, wounds, tortures, and humiliates innocents, particularly when they are of a colored race.

James Russell Lowell wrote of our propensity for such acts in *The Biglow Papers*, which dealt with his opposition to the Mexican-American War:

> . . . I hed a strong persuasion
> Thet Mexicans worn't human beans,
>   —an ourang outang nation,
> A sort o' folks a chap could kill an' never
>   dream on 't arter,
> No more 'n a feller 'd dream o' pigs thet
>   he hed hed to slarter;
> I'd an idee thet they were built arter the
>   darkie fashion all,
> An' kickin' colored folks about, you know,
>   's a kind o' national.[9]

In 1848 many Americans saw their own "Evil" lying within. The Mexican-American war was opposed for its racism. Abolitionists such as William Lloyd Garrison burned with fervor against the cruelties of slavery. When America does such despicable things today, we find a few scapegoats, rap them on the knuckles as we did William Calley over My Lai, as we do now with enlisted men and women, the torturers of Muslim prisoners, ignoring the officers who commanded them. Then we continue on our way, smugly believing that we have "taken care of the problem," that these soldiers have only exhibited aberrant behavior.

Over the years of reading and writing I learned the hard truth of America as a nation that has committed its own sins of repression and barbarity. We were not the "pure" people of God so many claimed. Our "shining city on a hill" had a dark cloud over it. We should not only blame others for their sins.

~~≈~~

Another fact of history I learned was that the rise of Hitler and the Holocaust was far more complex than we usually assumed. Our interpretation of the Holocaust seldom goes back to World War I and the years that followed it.

The defeat of Germany and the huge casualties in European countries bred an anger, especially among those defeated, that helped cause World War II. The Versailles Treaty of 1919 with its fallacies and hard demands on the defeated nations was partially an act of revenge as well as a return to colonialism. Its conditions helped set the framework for the rise of Hitler and the tragic fact of World War II. Hitler and his supporters viewed the Versailles Treaty of 1919 with its reparations and its shrinking of Germany's borders as, perhaps, the main cause of the collapse of Germany in the 1920s. The terrible depression that so destroyed the economy exacerbated their rage. Jews were labeled "traitors" who stabbed Germany and the "fallen soldier," the real hero of World War I, in the back. Hitler offered the Germans a way to rediscover dignity with the Jews as the scapegoat to blame for massive national fail-

ure. The causes for Hitler's rise to power were buried in these years before 1933.

The failure to stop Hitler also lay in the inability of the victors—England, France, Italy, and the
United States—to form an international organization that might have prevented future wars. These
nations attempted to create that organization at the
end of World War I, the League of Nations. The
League would deal with recalcitrant countries whose
aim was aggrandizement, aggression, and war.
However, the League was never ceded the powers
necessary to perform these duties and, in 1919, the
United States gave this international effort to reach
peace another grievous blow. The U.S. Senate refused to ratify it, denying President Wilson's commitment to the League. The League, therefore, never
effectively dealt with Hitler's acts of aggression in
the 1930s.

It was at this point in my long effort to understand European history that I began to formulate an
answer to those who asked "What about Hitler?"
those who held to the apocalyptic thinking that dic-
tators must be met only with the threat of war.

In one way I knew those who asked this question were absolutely right in their conviction that
World War II was a just war against "Evil." And, of
course, I agreed with them and always would; I had
almost paid my life for that agreement. In 1935 Hitler
had repudiated the Treaty of Versailles; that year the
German Reichstag passed the Nuremburg Laws,
denying many civil rights to Jews; in 1936 Hitler occupied the Rhineland; in the spring of 1938 Germany
took Austria. In September of that year, as Gorton
Carruth, Jr., wrote in *World Facts and Dates*, "The
democracies, represented by France and Great Britain, agreed in the Munich Pact to Adolf Hitler's demands and advised Czechoslovakia to surrender part

of its territory to Nazi Germany. Neville Chamberlain, prime minister of Great Britain, returned home, saying the Munich Pact meant 'peace in our time.' Others saw the agreement as appeasement, peace at any price that would only lead to more demands from Hitler."[10] Of course, they were right.

So the first and simplest part of the answer to those who ask that question about Hitler must be: the West accommodated Hitler, and so he invaded more nations and took greater power from 1935 to 1939. Apocalyptic thinking must thus reject all thoughts of appeasement. The "Evil" dictator must be stopped. There can be no compromise with those who intend great harm.

And yet in another way those who give this answer to the rise of Hitler are completely wrong. Not bothering to examine the history of the 1920s and early 1930s in Europe they fail to see that Hitler might have been stopped in his meteoric rise to power. If there had been less revenge and repression in the treaties ending World War I, if an international organization with real power had been created, there would have been less chance for Hitler to rise and, perhaps, no Hitler to appease.

Thus, the rise of Hitler and the memory of World War I and the years between the wars have a far greater complexity than admitted by those who point only to appeasement as the cause of Germany's aggression in World War II. We have simplified that complex history with the myth "When Evil Lies in Others, War Is the Means to Justice." We need to learn a new equation: that war may not bring justice; instead, unintended consequences and the corruption of both the defeated and victor follow war.

~⬎~

Even our current mess in Iraq goes back to our inability to read world history. That same Versailles Treaty of 1919 and other treaties and deals that followed, organized the whole region of the Middle East into new nations and distributed them as mandates to the victorious European powers. This was a betrayal of pledges made to the Arab leaders of the Middle East, who had fought with the Allies against Turkey and the Germans, and had been promised their independence after Allied victory. But France got Syria and Lebanon and England received Palestine, Transjordan and Iraq as mandates while Saudi Arabia and Turkey were given independence. Margaret MacMillan describes the formation of Iraq in *Paris, 1919*:

> In 1919 there was no Iraq people; history, religion, geography pulled the people apart, not together. Basra looked south, toward India and the Gulf; Baghdad had strong links with Persia; and Mosul had closer ties with Turkey and Syria. . . . The population was about half Shia Muslim and a quarter Sunni. . . . The cities were relatively advanced and cosmopolitan; in the countryside, hereditary tribal and religious leaders still dominated. . . . There was no Iraqi nationalism. . . . For the Arabs, 1920 remains the year of disaster. . . . Railway lines were cut and towns besieged; British officers were murdered. The British reacted harshly, sending punitive expeditions across the land to burn villages and exact fines. . . . Their aircraft machine-gunned and bombed from the air.[11]

And in a column for the *Los Angeles Times*, Alex Cockburn wrote:

> The Royal Air Force asked Winston Churchill, then the secretary of state for war, for permission to use chemical weapons. . . . Churchill wrote: "I do not understand squeamishness about the use of gas. I am strongly in favor of using poisoned gas against uncivilized tribes. . . . We cannot in any circumstance acquiesce in the non-utilization of any weapons which are available to procure a speedy termination to the disorder which prevails on the frontier.[12]

One consequence of the treaties following World War I was an Iraq that never really worked. Iraq was thrown together, composed of several religious sects (Shiites and Sunnis) and ethnicities (Kurds and Arabs), people who actually loathed each other. The Sunnis dominated. To rein in rebellious Shiites Winston Churchill actually considered bombing their villages with poison gas, though he was overruled. We considered none of this history when we declared war on Iraq. We see now the terrible chaos that results from trying to form one nation from those whose hate is centuries old.

We engage in apocalyptic thinking when we ignore these historic realities that so impact how we struggle with this new threat of terrorism that takes the form of shadowy individuals, outside of nation states, who wish to do us in. There are hard lessons from World War I that might have kept us from the dilemmas we now face in Iraq, in the Middle East. If we had understood the role of the Versailles Treaty and other treaties in laying the base for the rise of Hitler and forming a cobbled nation in Iraq, if we had not feared appeasement, we might not have so quickly tossed away the idea of cooperation with all nations of the world to defeat terrorist activity after 9/11.

~~∾~~

Perhaps former President George H. W. Bush, also a combat veteran of World War II, and the current president's father, spoke for much of my generation when he wrote in a December 1990 letter to his five children, "How many lives might have been saved if appeasement had given way to force earlier in the late 30s or earliest 40s? How many Jews might have been spared the gas chambers, or how many Polish patriots might be alive today? I look at today's crisis [Saddam's invasion of Kuwait] as 'good' vs. 'evil'—yes, it is that clear."[13] President H. W. Bush's letter demonstrates both apocalyptic thinking and a lack of understanding of European history. His letter ignores all that happened in Europe prior to the '30s as the time Hitler might have been stopped. Neither he nor any of the newer leaders of America (including his son) seem to understand that many of the real causes of Hitler's rise lie in World War I and the way the Versailles Treaty ended it. If we understood this, then we might begin to be able to separate the concept of appeasement from that of compromise and cooperation.

As long as apocalyptic thinking so dominates our understanding of the world, compromise is impossible and warfare becomes our way of life as we constantly hunt for another "Evil" to be eradicated by our own goodness and purity. We will never be able to have good intelligence about those we oppose. The belief in their satanic power will pervert whatever knowledge we gain of their true intent.

Clearly this is what happened with Saddam Hussein; just as clearly, we now understand that the power of the USSR and the Communist Party in the United States were also overinflated by our fears of the dark "enemy" who would destroy us.

~◈~

Our task today is to struggle to understand why other nations act as they do when they also treat their people in cruel and barbaric ways, instead of immediately frightening them with the threat of war. If we understood their reasons for so acting, it just might be possible to determine areas of agreement between us. We might discover that there are some ways we can cooperate such as in solutions to problems of worldwide environmental degradation of air and water quality. In so cooperating the leaders and people of these nations might become human to us instead of symbols of "Evil."

We also might look at their history to see the causes for their brutality and in those causes—from repression to poverty—we might discover some other reasons for understanding the way they act. Again, we might reach small degrees of cooperation if we but started with an assumption other than that they are the "enemy" and always "Evil" and so must be attacked.

Can we, at last, finally learn that "Evil" lies in ourselves as well as others, that World War II had other causes besides appeasement? Can we do away with our beliefs in apocalyptic thinking, acting as though our purity was the only answer for the world? Can we realize that making war in this modern era will always involve killing innocents and causing atrocities, always release dark, destructive, and corrupt emotions deep within ourselves?

It is time for us to understand that it was completely sensible for the citizens of Europe to say "no" to the war in Iraq and President Bush's unilateral attack there. The memories of the murderous qualities of a war that began in 1914 and ended in 1945 ran too deep for them to easily accept apocalyptic thinking and the idea of a war that might trigger even greater conflagrations. It is time to begin to work in concert and cooperation with other nations to discover new ways of thinking and acting beyond the Myths of World War II. As long as we believe that evil lies in others and that war is the only means to justice, we will continue to wreak havoc on the world.

It is time for us to change.[14]

Part V

Beyond the Myths of World War II

CHAPTER 10

New Ways of Thinking and Acting

So what are my conclusions from my search for an understanding of the role of the Myths of World War II in America? They are ones I scarcely wish to acknowledge, loving this country as I still do. After all, I volunteered to protect it and still carry shrapnel inside me from that act. I am still certain that the Declaration of Independence, the Constitution, and the Bill of Rights are three of the most significant political documents ever written. Yet what I have learned leads me to doubt my faith and my sacrifice: our dedication to the Myths of World War II has led the United States to maintain the most warlike posture and to develop the most powerful military on the globe since 1945.

How do we compare to other nations in these long decades of bloodshed since 1945?

Iraq, Iran, and North Korea were labeled by President Bush the "axis of evil." The wars they have fought since 1945 have been brutal: Iraq's use of poison gas against Iran and the Kurds, its wholesale repression of the Shiites; Iran's bitter retaliation against Iraq, its harsh treatment of its dissidents, its position on the Holocaust and Israel, and its quest

for military and atomic power; North Korea's surprise attack on South Korea, its barbaric treatment
of American prisoners, its acquisition of atomic
weaponry, and its authoritarian repression of those
who dissent. China? After the communists won the
civil war, it seized Tibet, joined the North Koreans
in the Korean War, brutalized its citizens in the Cultural Revolution and, later, repressed students at
Tiananmen Square. England? France? They were
with us in the Korean War, then England continued
its thousand year battle in Ireland and fought the
Falklands War. France had its struggles in Vietnam,
then Algeria. England joins us now in Iraq but France
has kept itself free from such war-making actions.
Germany, Japan? Defeated in World War II, they have
turned to ways of peace. The USSR, now Russia?
We defeated them in the forty-year Cold War but they
had their invasion of Afghanistan and now their
struggle with the Chechens continues in its brutality, though they opposed our invasion of Iraq.

There are also the bloodstains in Israel and in
Palestine and in the Middle East, the genocides in
Rwanda, the Sudan, and Cambodia; the conflagration in the Congo; the wars between India and Paki-
stan; the bloody repressions in the Far East and the
Horn of Africa. The list repeats itself in monotonous
and awful successions, a world gone mad with killings and wedded to the latest weapons technology.

But America has not kept apart from such
bloodletting. We were in a Cold War for over forty of
the past sixty years, which led to our panoply of
weapons, far superior to those of other nations. For
more than twenty of those years we fought in overt
wars. Since 1945 these wars have taken our troops
into Korea, Vietnam, Lebanon, Grenada, Panama,
the Gulf War, Somalia, Kosovo, Bosnia and Serbia,
Afghanistan, and Iraq. It is estimated that we killed

"perhaps three million" civilians in our bombing in the Vietnam War.[1] In the same decades, we supported, sometimes covertly, authoritarian regimes in Guatemala, Iran, El Salvador, Nicaragua, and Chile. We have sent troops into the Dominican Republic, Haiti, and Colombia. We now have troops stationed in sixty-two nations.[2] Approximately four hundred thousand of our young men and women have been killed or wounded as members of the armed forces since 1945, and that total keeps rising in Afghanistan and Iraq.[3] In all these conflicts we, or the troops we supported, have killed, wounded or injured millions of innocent civilians. As I write, bitter warfare rages in Iraq. We caused widespread destruction in the city of Fallujah in a battle reminiscent of the street firefighting in France and Germany in World War II. Our actions in such cities are as devastating to them as Hurricane Katrina was to New Orleans in 2005.

The difference between the United States and all other warring nations is simple: we won World War II without our land or civilians being seriously hurt. Out of that war we were the nation that triumphed, that became the most powerful nation in all history, arching over the other nations of the world. Devotion to arms has become our way of life since that victory, supported by the largest military budget in the world, the most atomic and hydrogen bombs in the world, the greatest arsenal of other weapons in the world, and the highest arms exports to other nations in the world.[4] Leading the world in the development of weapons, we force other nations to run after us with their weapons programs. The arms race over the world consumes monies that might be used for the poor, the hungry, and the ill. We did not even pause after the ruthless attacks of 9/11 to consider other alternatives beyond that same brutal application of force learned in World War II.

The Myths of World War II have become our guides, our reference points.

The lives of three generations of Americans have now been irrevocably changed by World War II, the wars of Korea, Vietnam, and Iraq, and all the little wars in between. Our domestic life and our economy are interwoven with the consequences of our dedication to war, our foreign policy a function of our military prowess.

These myths have just led us into one more war. Both the general public and its leaders are beginning to see the mess that these Myths of World War II have made for us in Iraq. Calls from Congress to bring home our troops from Iraq intensify. For the first time, more than fifty percent of the public registers opposition to the war.[5] These are but echoes of those cries so long ago to end the "police action" in Korea or the war in Vietnam. What we simply do not seem to grasp is that our war-making lies in our allegiance to the Myths of World War II. They support our faith that our arms are the one way to solve our problems in the world. When another threat frightens us (as I fear it will), or when we discover another "enemy" (as I'm sure we will) and immediately name it a satanic power, patriotic fervor will explode again, war will be declared, and that newest enemy will feel the full force of our might. Once more, we will become mired in a war without victory, costing lives of our young people, of innocents, injuring the morale of our armed forces, and spending public dollars we cannot afford. A fourth and a fifth generation of soldiers will then suffer. As a people we are now so influenced—I almost wrote "controlled"— by our dedication to and acceptance of the Myths of World War II that it is likely new wars lie ahead.

Thus, the issue today is not just the simple one—how can we leave Iraq?—but, rather one far more difficult: how can we turn from war as the solution to our international problems? How can we finally grow beyond the fierce control of those myths over our national unconscious so that, at last, we lead ourselves and the world toward ways of real peace? How can we change? *Can* we change?

Three quotations are relevant as I raise these questions. Two are new. One I have used elsewhere in this book and it needs to be repeated here. In an essay in *Combat, the Distant Drum Was Still,* Capt. Laurence Critchell tells us of what happened in the aftermath of World War II:

> For this strange state of mind which fell upon us for a little while after the guns had been silenced was a vague sense of obscenity. It was the faint, lingering aftertaste of having achieved something monstrous. We had unleashed powers beyond our comprehension. Entire countries lay waste beneath our hands—and, in the doing of it, our hands were forever stained. It was of no avail to tell ourselves that we had done what we had to do, the only thing we could have done. It was enough to know we had done it. We had turned the evil of our enemies back upon them a hundredfold and, in so doing, something of our own integrity had been shattered, had been irrevocably lost.[6]

Ernest Hemingway in *For Whom the Bell Tolls* writes movingly of the central moral problem of war, killing, in the Spanish Civil War, precursor to World War II. His peasant hero, Anselmo, meditates:

All that I am sorry for is the killing. . . . after the war there will have to be some great penance done for the killing. . . . there must be some form of civic penance organized that all may be cleansed from the killing or else we will never have a true and human basis for living. The killing is necessary, I know, but still the doing of it is very bad for a man and I think that, after all this is over and we have won the war, there must be a penance of some for the cleansing of us all.[7]

And Paul Fussell's observation, taken from his book *Wartime*, and quoted in chapter four, sums up the terrible problem we face: "America has not yet understood what the Second World War was like and has thus been unable to use such understanding to re-interpret and re-define the national reality and to arrive at something like public maturity."[8]

To arrive at that public maturity, to admit the shame that Captain Critchell speaks of, to attain some understanding of and penance for all the killings we have done in these decades, means we must reach deep into ourselves, into the soul of America, and begin to change those parts of our national character that are so dedicated to the Myths of World War II.

We must not stop at simply leaving Iraq and admitting our errors there. We see the terrible failure these myths have created for our nation in Iraq, their cost to our troops, to innocents, to the reputation and morale of our armed forces, to our worldwide reputation, and to our pocketbooks. We must understand that it is not new policies and programs, strategies and tactics, more powerful demonstrations, longer petitions, more civil disobedience, or a reformed army we require. Rather the problem of changing our allegiance to the Myths of World War II and our dedication to war lies far deeper than such surface proposals. We need to form new values about war in America and then initiate ways of thinking and acting so as to reach those values.

For many years I scoffed at the hope that it might be possible for this country to turn from war. Our centuries-old dedication to its myths, our incessant use of arms, our patriotic rumblings whenever we are threatened—why, any change seemed preposterous. Yet, with age and a deeper knowledge of American history, I understand that, in at least one instance, the deeply held convictions of Americans about an institution as pernicious as war—slavery— were overturned. New values, new thought patterns, and action ended an injustice as powerfully imbedded in the national consciousness as our dedication to war.

Opposition to slavery began in the early days of colonial settlement. In 1688 Mennonites in Germantown, Pennsylvania, passed a resolution condemning it. Quakers in that state also protested the practice. John Woolman in the eighteenth century reported in his *Journal,* one of the first important pieces of American literature, his opposition to slavery. The Constitution allowed the importation of slaves for twenty years after its ratification. It counted a slave as three-fifths of a person for the purpose of a census to determine the population of a state. In 1790 the issue of slavery was once again forced on the federal government: "On February 11, 1790 two Quaker delegations, one from New York and the other from Philadelphia, presented petitions to the House calling for the federal government to put an immediate end to the African slave trade." That petition was substantially rewritten by The House, its original meaning gutted. The struggle against slavery in terms of government action was effectively ended for many years after that legislative battle.[9]

But the abolition movement continued its opposition to slavery in ways that changed the nation. In the 1830s and 1840s that movement was given force by small numbers of men and women who founded newspapers, spoke publicly, volunteered in the underground railroad, and raised, in the profoundest way, the moral question of slavery: the degradation of one human being by another. Those objections caught fire and eventually consumed a practice that had been common to America for over two hundred years, since long before its founding as a nation, and to the rest of the world for thousands of years.

This movement was started by men and women in all levels of society: Quakers at the fringes, women from the feminist movement, aristocrats and businessmen of Boston, expatriate Southerners such as the Grimké sisters, former slaves like Frederick Douglass and Sojurner Truth. Some possessed great status and power, others were radical reformers. This movement was often fueled from below, from citizens in cities, small towns, and rural areas, from leaders who sprang from the simplest roots like William Lloyd Garrison who said, "I have the need to be all on fire, for I have mountains of ice about me to melt."[10] The movement began in the hope that non-violence might free those slaves. Finally, it ended in a bitter war, as all other efforts to free African Americans had failed.

Then, one hundred years later, once again leaders rose from the people: Rosa Parks, whose resistance sparked a civil rights rebellion; Martin Luther King, Jr., with his cry "I have a dream." And this time freedom, some modicum of it, was reached with civil resistance but without war. These leaders and their followers created new values and new ways of thinking and acting about civil rights for African Americans.

The awful costs of war I have examined in this book and the fact that a majority of Americans now question our war in Iraq make me hope that the voices of opposition to war and its myths are ready to rise again as they did in 1945–46. In sixty years we have expended too many lives and too much money on causes that have proved false and intelligence that has proven to be a lie. It is time to confront the nation with our sadness and our anger over America's dedication to the Myths of World War II. It is time to bring those myths into the spotlight. Long decades of killing and wounding our young people and innocents all over the world are enough.

We need a most simple pledge: "It is a sin to kill a child."

As I meditate on that pledge, I can hear those surging voices that tell me the moment for this change may be approaching just as the moment to end slavery finally arrived. Those voices rise from the great gatherings of people around the world who demonstrated against the war in Iraq. They come from that 50-plus percent of Americans who have now turned against that war, a far cry from the 80 percent of Americans who believed, when I started this book, that war equals justice. They are represented by those columnists who consistently attack the war for its hypocrisy and its brutalization of the human being; they come from organizations such as MoveOn.org, the American Friends Service Committee, the Friends Committee on National Legislation, and the Fellowship of Reconciliation, that consistently oppose war. They come from the words of

178   Worshipping the Myths of World War II

bloggers and of listservs that flood the electronic world with messages against war.

These are the same cries for peace I heard in 1945 and 1946 at the end of World War II when the whole world had been so badly hurt. The longing after World War II among men and women and children for a peaceful world was but an echo of the dreams the citizens of the earth had in 1919. This desire for peace lies deep in the heart of humanity, a hope never lost but always returning, generation after generation.

This longing has many parts. It is built of compassion, of being able to feel the pain of another. It is built of fear, the fear of losing one's life, one's home, and one's family. It is built of rage, anger over what men do to each other and especially to children. It is built of moral indignation: it is simply wrong to kill a child. It is built out of an understanding of unintended consequences: the killing of innocents that we ask our soldiers to do affects them over a lifetime. This longing calls no generation "great" that fights a war, admires no stories of combat, and recognizes that war is a tragedy for all who fight it, corrupting both those at the front and those behind it. It understands that war breeds atrocity. It knows the great cost of war, wasted resources that could instead save the sick, the elderly, the young, and the poor. It sorrows for the lost, the lonely, and the hurt, those who never recover from the losses of war.

This longing is a delicate feeling, one so easily bruised. It must be nourished carefully so it is not crushed again as it was in 1919 and in 1945–46. If it survives, then perhaps it might spread slowly over America and challenge our dedication to war as, once, we were challenged about our dedication to slavery. Challenge war not just in the way we vote or run the federal government or the way we spend our money on the military or on foreign policy but challenge it in our deepest heart, fomenting a revolution in the values we have about war and the way we live and think and act in twenty-first-century America.

~∼~

Ways of nurturing these emerging peaceful feelings that are accessible to the ordinary citizen are required. Instead of occasional demonstrations and petitions, what is needed are modes of thinking and acting that individuals and communities can pursue on a daily basis. But these suggestions must begin modestly. Too many articles, too many reports, too many sermons have said, "war is wrong." And nothing has happened.

A few proposals for this change:

As a nation we need to learn that the four Myths of World War II exist and mask the truths of war. We need to understand how the myths control us and exert an unconscious force when we fear an enemy by seizing our emotions and directing us to make war. Our decisions to declare war are often not in our real interest but instead are driven by these myths. Unmasking them is a national task that is good for our public health. When the threat of war arrives we need to ask ourselves: what is this war's real source? What will be its real costs? What emotions are actually at work within us to so worship this particular war? Is our enemy real or the product of our imagination? What might be the unintended consequences of the proposed war? Who will profit? Who will lose? We need to understand that killing and wounding, not heroism or glory, are the true consequences of war—killing in all its ruthlessness up front and in the face of the enemy, killing in all its impersonality, done from the air fifteen thousand feet above where deaths and wounds are imposed on helpless civilians. When possible, we need to revive the idea of penance for that killing and understand the terrible pain we, as a society, inflict on innocents. We need to call particular attention to those wounded in flesh or spirit for they are the ones who truly bear the burdens of war. We need to recognize the cost they will pay for their entire lives.

To understand the enormous hold the myths of war have over us, we need to question the certainty that evil always lies in others, never in ourselves, and our apocalyptic thinking that American force is the way to eradicate evil. If we accept our responsibility for being a partial cause of the violence in today's world we might reach different conclusions about ways to act, seeing compromise, cooperation, or law enforcement as proper steps instead of defining them as appeasement. We have been driven far too long by the myth derived from the memory of the Holocaust that evil always lies outside ourselves, in others, while we are "pure." We are unable to accept our own part in the violence that so haunts the world, what we did in World War II and since then our interference in nations everywhere. If we can accept our responsibility for the pain and havoc we have spread over the globe with our warlike actions, then, perhaps, new solutions to war might yet be found.

We must pay much greater attention to the ancient and unconscious process of scapegoating. We need to ask if the newest enemy actually is a scapegoat. When we are attacked or hurt, our instant reaction is to strike at the most convenient target even when that target is not to blame. Our rage can only be satisfied by destroying another person or place or thing. In the South after its defeat in the Civil War, young black males were lynched. In France the poor woman who slept with Germans was punished. After World War II, the United States and the Soviet Union blamed each other, leading the world into the Cold War. After 9/11 it was Iraq. Such rapid responses are often not in our best interest; instead they create immense pain and often make unsolvable long-range problems. To ask whether the person or country we blame for our latest disaster is really at fault is, perhaps, the first step toward the new public maturity that Paul Fussell seeks.

All these proposals merge into the greatest lesson we need to learn if we and the world are to survive the kinds of weapons we have produced: the ability to distinguish real enemies from enemies who are but products of our imagination. It is true that some times real enemies exist and that we as a nation, as a people, and as individuals must be ready to protect ourselves against them. The challenge is not to waste ourselves and our resources on imagined enemies by preparing and fighting wars that should never be. Now the slightest twitch in another country far smaller than America is seen as a threat of war. The four myths of war surge from our subconscious. We arm ourselves in mighty force to overcome our newest enemy, ready to smash it to smithereens. Our intelligence—as in the case of Iraq and the USSR before it—overinflates the force of the opposition. Our paranoia takes over and we live in fear. Certainly, there are real enemies to arm against. But our problem is to know them, not to make enemies out of shadows. We must be prepared for the real enemy, but we must admit that few of our enemies are ever real.

We need massive support for research into new thinking on the nature of the Myths of World War II, on the "enemy," and on issues of peace and war. We need to expand our critical thinking about the war film, war movie, and war book, both novel and non-fiction. Six books published in recent years come to mind as examples of the new thinking we need: *Afterwar* by Lori Grinker; *War Is a Force that Gives Us Meaning* by Christopher Hedges; *A Terrible Love of War* by James Hillman; *Homefront* by Catherine Lutz; *In the Shadow of War* by Michael S. Sherry; and *Just War* by Howard Zinn. We need to rediscover the movies of our past that question war's myths—*All Quiet on the Western Front, Gallipoli,* and *Breaker Morant*—and make such movies again today instead of those that romanticize war. Newer books and films must explore what war really is in a post-industrial, post-modern society. They must struggle to defeat the attractions of the Myths of World War II in ways seldom approached. We need a society and a culture that supports such creative endeavors.

This research must impact television and video games as critically as it does films, memoirs, and books. Our youth become disposed to violence and killing by the images we give them on television and in their video games. In a real way we have created visual images that appeal to the lowest common denominator of the human being. Only mighty cries of rage and disgust, and refusal to buy the products of those who romanticize the myths of war, can bring about the change needed in the way we worship those myths and the images they produce.

In this research we need to discover a language of peace. More often than not we define peace as merely the absence of war and violence, not as a creative and binding force that gives meaning to communal and personal lives. We have little understanding of how many kinds of peace there are in the world. There is the difference between personal and institutional peace. There is the peace we feel as individuals with family, friends, loved ones. There is neighborhood and communal peace, peace between nations, peace among nations. More than likely each of these aspects of peace has a different quality; each requires a new thought or new word to encompass it. How can we give up the myths of war and seek peace if we do not even understand what it is?

Part of this research needs to consider those whom I call Patriots of Peace, presented in my other books. There is a hidden tradition in America of those who have given their lives and careers for ways of peace. They are heroes and heroines of a different type. We need to study them in school; we need to understand and honor them. After all, some of the first peace societies in world history were formed in the United States.

We must also examine a problem never solved, seldom even approached. How are the criticisms and fallacies of the four Myths of World War II to be made attractive to those outside the "chorus"? Do the traditional actions of peace groups—the demonstrations, the petitions, the picketing—ever reach the uncertain, the unconvinced, the warlike? What are the best methods to bring about a reasonable discussion of war in America?

But it is not enough to simply think about these myths and develop new ways of understanding them. Actions are required, actions that we can take both on our own and in concert to change our dedication to war. A few of these follow:

Most of us have little control over these great issues of war and peace. But we do have some control over our daily lives. And so we should begin the effort of changing our dedication to war with the acts we can control: the way we treat those we love, our friends, our neighbors, our acquaintances, our subordinates, our peers, and our bosses. As mentioned earlier in this book, since the end of World War II, a vast decline in all kinds of civil behavior has occurred in the United States. Rage, raunchiness, and a constant aggression seem to be our daily fare. But each of us has the opportunity to act in a different way, and this is perhaps the most important contribution we can make, our most important testament to peace. If we act in more peaceful ways, if we take moments in the day to be pleasant, gentle, and kind instead of competitive, aggressive, and hard, then a different way of living in America might be born.

We also live in a community. In his fine book *Bowling Alone*, Robert D. Putnam both revives and invents forms of communal relations. All increase what he calls social capital, the ability to live in a mutually helpful, peaceful, and humane community. He presents methods that would turn us from the myths of war at the neighborhood and community scale. He mentions six spheres of action that might change the way Americans relate to each other in the twenty-first century: "youth and schools; the workplace; urban and metropolitan design; religion; arts and culture; and politics and government."[11]

I strongly recommend that his proposals for new forms of community and social capital be included in efforts to change our ways of acting about the dedication to war in America. If we can live together peacefully in a community, it is far more likely we can live together peacefully in the nation and in the world.

There are other actions local communities can take to question war and its myths. In the build-up to the war in Iraq, city councils from Santa Cruz, California, to Cambridge, Massachusetts, met and voted for resolutions opposing the war. The debate explored all aspects of the proposed war in Iraq. Local governments might well consider a continuing role in monitoring the war power of the federal government as a way to educate local publics.

Discussions at the local level can also provide non-threatening forums for citizens to express their opinions on war and on the Myths of World War II. As the Iraq war started, I gave a few workshops in local churches and learned of the enormous desire of citizens to find a neutral place where they could explore their thoughts and feelings about both the war and the threat of terrorism. Many seemed reluctant to express reservations in public, feeling such expressions were unpatriotic. Providing workshops in which all opinions are respected and held in confidence would be a great contribution toward civil discourse in America when war is threatened.

But it is the federal government that makes war, so it is also essential to change the way it takes us into war. On December 8, 1941, the day after Pearl Harbor, President Roosevelt went to Congress and asked for a declaration of war, which Congress immediately gave him. Since then, wars have come into being through executive fiat with Congress playing a minor role. Every administration since the beginning of the Cold War has expanded the war powers of the president and Congress has supported these actions with legislation, budgets, and declarations giving power to the executive branch. Presidents and their administrations always claim that in times as dangerous as ours instantaneous actions may be required in order to protect the nation, allowing no time for debate. Such swiftness often leads to disaster, as in Vietnam and Iraq; speed is a prescription for failure. False or trumped-up intelligence has been used and may be used again to buttress the decision. In Article I, Section 8, the Constitution clearly gives the Congress the right "to declare war." If Congress would exercise this right again, show some courage, do its own investigation, and ask more pointed questions about any war proposed by any administration, then wrongful wars might not occur—or at least be less frequent.

It is also appropriate to consider improved methods for declaring war. In the 1970s Congress required that environmental impact statements should accompany proposed land developments. These statements encompass the economic, physical, and environmental costs and benefits of the proposed development. The nature of war has changed so drastically since the Constitution was adopted in 1787 that declarations of war might best be based on a war impact statement which would define the nature of the enemy, state the purpose of the war, describe, review, and criticize the intelligence on which the war is based, outline the methods of conducting the war, project its probable costs—economic, environmental, and social, evaluate the impact on the military and on innocent civilians, including the downside of the proposed war, estimate the number of casualties, propose exit strategies, and suggest alternatives to war. If Congress had conducted such an intensive exercise before the war in Iraq, there may well have been no war. We have largely forgotten that our founding fathers formed three separate branches of government in the Constitution.

Another Congressional responsibility found in Article I, Section 8, of the Constitution is "to raise and support armies." If we follow the proposals above, especially in our understanding of "enemies" and our turning from apocalyptic thinking, then slowly, over time, our defense budget should decline. Congress will face the hard responsibility of determining how to use funds no longer meant for war. Currently, expenditures by the Department of Defense impact all Americans in unknown and unstudied ways. Military bases help support whole metropolitan areas. Contracts of all kinds from producing rifles to bullets to MREs keep much of our economy thriving. No-bid contracts support the Halliburtons of America. Outsourcing of tasks once thought to belong to the military from guarding high officials to truck driving—remember the Red Ball Express of World War II?—lets individuals take jobs at ten times the amount paid the soldier. Patience and wisdom will allow workers, so long dependent on defense dollars, to be trained for peacetime jobs and so survive the transition. If we turn from the Myths of World War II we must also slowly give up our mighty dedication to the building of arms and the selling of them abroad, an effort that may take decades.

As we distinguish real from imagined enemies, reduce armed forces so as to meet only real threats, develop ways to cut back defense budgets, and use the savings for other purposes, we might begin to appreciate how, since the end of World War II, a wealth of cooperative endeavors to prevent war, seek peace, protect human rights, and widen human opportunities have slowly been built over the globe. The Friends Committee on National Legislation reported in *Peaceful Prevention of Deadly Conflict*:

> A growing body of research is contributing to a global movement for the peaceful prevention of deadly conflict . . . [it includes] the report of the Carnegie Commission on Preventing Deadly Conflict in 1998 . . . the Secretary General's *Report on the Prevention of Armed Conflict* and

the report *Responsibility to Protect* . . .
[these] marked important steps in the
world community's effort to better understand, predict, and prevent the outbreak
of violent conflict.[12]

Over the past fifty-plus years, the world, la-
boriously and inefficiently, has slowly learned
how to prevent acts of violence before they
occur by acting together in concert, not as
nations apart in preemptive strikes. All these
efforts take us beyond the myths of war, beyond preemption, and lead us toward international cooperation.

Our "War on Terror" presents an opportunity for such cooperation. However,
we have chosen a different model, rooted
in the Myths of World War II. In over four
years we have learned that this model really doesn't work. The same macabre story
is repeated each day: deaths and woundings
of our soldiers and their civilians; infrastructure destroyed; nations in chaos and
fear; Bali, Spain, England attacked. There
will be no end to it until "victory" occurs.
And yet no one seems to know what victory means.

I asked at the beginning of this book if war
was the best means to pursue our self-interest in this new kind of struggle with single
and savage individuals willing to die as they
destroy the " infidel." Does war only enflame
them to commit even more barbaric suicide
bombings?

We have learned the answer. The Myths of World War II have led us deeper into hate and hate increases the ferocity of the terrorist. It is time to admit we made a mistake and turn from war and its myths in our struggle with terrorists, time to treat them as other nations do, as criminals, and not dignify them as warriors, time to ask what causes their rage and their hatred of us. It is time to stop torture, rendition, and the concentration camp. It is time to understand that the causes of terrorism lie in poverty, ill-health, abusive regimes, uneven distribution of income, and struggles over natural resources, particularly, oil. It is time to admit that war but encourages those Muslims committed to jihad. It is time to seek international, cooperative solutions to their violence. The mighty war machine we developed out of our victory in World War II has shown itself as inadequate to this task. We need police work at an international level—international law and courts and justice—combined with the search for causes so as to reach the roots of rage and deal directly with them. These are the tools we need to form a peaceful world beyond the Myths of World War II.

~~~

Voices call for that peace from all nations. Though still muted, they are ready to explode in a mighty hymn, a chorus of all tongues demanding life beyond the myths of war. The multitudes who have really experienced war or who understand its consequences are ready to speak. And they will be heard in the coming years. It is our responsibility as Americans to help them, for we are the most powerful nation and people in the world. We have the awesome responsibility of stopping the agony of industrial warfare that nations have suffered since August 1914.

But what I fear, fear so desperately, is that, just as the abolition of slavery required a civil war, it may take another war to lead us to the understanding of how dedicated we are to those myths. This new war could be our undoing. It could mute for another generation those voices crying for peace. It could become a conflagration that could burn the world, far beyond the horrors of World War II. When the war against terror is called World War III, when writers tell of World War IV with China, when the use of military power against Iran is discussed, the unintended costs of such wars are seldom mentioned.[13] The consequences of another world war on the United States could mean the same kind of devastation as World War II, the destruction in Europe increased a hundred fold and poured in molten flame on us, our children, and the children of the world.

Is it not far wiser, at last, for Americans to live by a sense of the good in humanity than continue our certainty in its "Evil?" Our founders recognized that men could compromise when they separated the powers in the Constitution, then passed the Bill of Rights. They proclaimed their faith that humanity, working together, could create a union of people, free and equal. It took long decades to end the evil of slavery. It took a bloody civil war to institute the faith in national unity. We still struggle with our acts of bias and our concentrations of inequality. Yet, that union has survived, our faith, our glory.

Is it not time, at last, for America to lead the

world beyond war and the belief in the "Evil" enemy toward a new union of all nations on earth, surely as difficult a task as the thirteen Colonies faced in 1775?[14] Is that not our task today? We have demanded that the Kurds, Sunnis, and Shiites so cooperate. Cannot we ask the same of all nations of the world? Of such "naive" desires was our union formed. Perhaps we can lead the community of nations toward this newer world.

In the McCarthy hearings of 1954, Joseph Welch finally stopped the ruthless charges of Joe McCarthy by facing him and asking, "Have you no sense of decency, sir, at long last? Have you no sense of decency?" Perhaps it is at last time to ask ourselves if we Americans have lost our sense of decency, our sense of shame, as we continue to try to rule the world with overwhelming force, killing and wounding our troops and innocent civilians. Once we were the most respected nation in the world. Now we are the most feared. The moment has come to change that perception of who we are by changing ourselves.

EPILOGUE

While I was writing this book, Bob Reed and Bill Montgomery died. Not a day passes that I do not long for them. I often stare at the phone, wishing I could ring their number. We used to joke about it: who would be the last one left?

Well, I got stuck with "the duty," as we said in the military. Maybe this book is the statement of that duty. I have tried to write as honestly as I could about what happened to all of us and to the world in World War II. I think Bob and Bill would have approved. In fact Bill wrote me a note of encouragement about my writing before he died and I would like to quote a little of it:

> We must, as you say so forcefully, find ways in which compassion can invade human commerce. We must find out how to believe that compassion rather than conquest is the better path to genetic survival.
>
> And you must help us. You cannot despair. We need you to push us along on this path. At the least, it will be a joyous experiment. It might even give our grandchildren new reasons to celebrate Thanksgiving.

I've struggled to meet Bill's request, to tell another story about World War II, one known to us who were in combat, whether for a day or a year, one known to us who lost friends, one known to us who lost parts of our body. It is the story we want to leave to our children and grandchildren: what war is truly like, not what new generations have made it out to be.

NOTES

Preface

1. Kevin Foster, *Fighting Fictions: War, Narrative, and National Identity* (London: Pluto Press, 1999), 3.
2. *Statistical Abstract of the United States, 2004–2005* (Washington, D.C.: U.S. Bureau of the Census), 332.
3. *World Almanac, 2005* (New York: World Almanac Books, 2005), 225.
4. Jack Shannon, "Cheney: New War Certain," *Rocky Mountain News*, February 13, 1992.
5. Robert Gildea, *Marianne in Chains: Daily Life in the Heart of France During the German Occupation* (New York: Metropolitan Books, 2002); W. G. Sebald, *On the Natural History of Destruction,* trans. Anthea Bell (New York: Random House, 2003).

Introduction

1. Robert Kagan, "A Tougher War for the U.S. Is One of Legitimacy," *New York Times,* January 24, 2004; Bob von Sternberg, "Armed Forces Enjoying Enduring Popularity," *Minneapolis Star Tribune,* May 26, 2003.
2. Gorton Carruth, Jr., *The Encyclopedia of American Facts and Dates* (New York: Harper Collins, 1997), 766, 790, 822, 834, 862; David Halberstam, *War in a Time of Peace* (New York: Scribner, 2001).
3. Victor Davis Hanson, *An Autumn of War: What America Learned From September 11 and the War on Terrorism* (New York: Anchor Books, 2002), 32, 104.

4. Max Boot, *The Savage Wars of Peace: Small Wars and the Rise of American Power* (New York: Basic Books, 2002), xix, xx.

5. Scott Simon, "Even Pacifists Must Support This War," *Wall Street Journal*, October 11, 2001.

6. Jill Abramson, "Bush Speaks of Heroism and Sacrifice at Cemetery in Normandy," *New York Times,* May 28, 2002.

7. Quoted in David E. Sanger, "Witness to Auschwitz Evil, Bush Draws a Lesson," *New York Times*, June 1, 2003.

8. Office of the Press Secretary, "National Security Advisor Condoleezza Rice Interview with ZDF German Television," July 31, 2003, available at www.whitehouse.gov/news/releases/2003/07.

9. The President of the United States, the *National Security Strategy* of the United States of America, September 2002.

10. Alexander Cockburn, "Bombs, the Moral Tools of the West," *Los Angeles Times,* February 3, 1991.

11. Margaret MacMillan, *Paris, 1919* (New York: Random House, 2003), 397; William R. Polk, *Understanding Iraq* (New York: Harper Collins, 2005), 67–101.

12. Hillary Clinton, "Addressing the National Security Challenges of Our Time: Fighting Terror and the Spread of Weapons of Mass Destruction," (lecture, the Brookings Institution, February 25, 2004, available at www.clinton.senate.gov/issues/nationalsecurity).

13. Robert Cooney and Helen Michalowski, *The Power of the People: Active Nonviolence in the United States* (Culver City, CA: Peace Press, 1977), 75.

14. Geoffrey Perret, *There's a War to Be Won: The United States Army in World War II;* (New York: Random House, 1991), 26; Russell F. Weigley, *Eisenhower's Lieutenants: The Campaign of France and Germany, 1944–1945* (Bloomington: Indiana University Press, 1981), 12.

15. Thomas Wolfe, *You Can't Go Home Again* (New York: Perennial Library, 1968), 48.

16. California State Military Museum, "California in World War II: The Shelling of Ellwood," www.militarymuseum.org/Ellwood.html.

17. *World Almanac, 2005* (New York: World Almanac Books, 2005), 227; *Statistical Abstract of the United States, 2000–2005* (Washington, D.C.: U.S. Bureau of the Census), 333; Peter Huchthausen, *America's Splendid Little Wars: A Short History of U.S. Military Engagements: 1975–2000* (New York: Viking/Penguin, 2003).

Chapter 1

1. Studs Terkel, *The Good War: An Oral History of World War II* (New York: The New Press, 1984), note at front.

2. John Keegan, *The Second World War* (New York: Viking Press, 1989), 590–91; Williamson Murray and Allan R. Millett, *A War To Be Won: Fighting the Second World War* (Cambridge, MA: Harvard University Press, 2000), 554–56; Peggy Saari and Aaron Maurice Saari, eds., *The Holocaust and World War II Almanac* (Detroit: Gale Group, 2001), 2:381–83; Alex Hook, *Illustrated History of the Third Reich* (Cobham, UK: TAJ Books, 2004), 226–33.

3. Hook, *Third Reich*, 232; Murray and Millett, *War to Be Won*, 554.

4. Saari and Saari, *Holocaust*, 382.

5. Sven Lindquist, *A History of Bombing* (New York: The New Press, 2001), 92–114; Peter Townsend, *Duel of Eagles* (New York: Simon and Schuster, 1971); Earl R. Beck, *Under the Bombs: The German Home Front, 1942–1945* (Lexington: University Press of Kentucky, 1986); Mark Anderson, "Crime and Punishment," *Nation* 281 (October 17, 2005): 31.

6. Christopher R. Browning, *Ordinary Men: Reserve Battalion 101 and the Final Solution in Poland* (New York: Harper Perennial, 1992).

7. Barbara Distel and Ruth Jakusch, eds., *Concentration Camp Dachau, 1933–1945,* trans. Jennifer Vernon, (Brussels: Comité International de Dachau, 1978), 82–83.

8. Christian Zentner and Friedemann Bedürftig, eds., *The Encyclopedia of the Third Reich*, trans. Amy Hackett, (New York: Macmillan, 1991), 2:728–30; I. C. B. Dear, ed., *The Oxford Companion to World War II* (Oxford: Oxford University Press, 1995), 913–15.

9. Iris Chang, *The Rape of Nanking* (New York: Penguin, 1997).

10. Beck, *Under the Bombs*, 69–70.

11. Chang, *The Rape of Nanking,* 59.

12. Richard Rhodes, *The Making of the Atomic Bomb* (New York: Simon and Schuster, 1986), 714–18.

13. Konnilyn G. Feig, *Hitler's Death Camps: The Sanity of Madness* (New York and London: Holmes & Meier Publishers, 1979), 67, 359–61; Lucy S. Dawidowicz, *The War Against the Jews: 1933–1945* (New York: Holt, Rinehart and Winston, 1975); Gerald Reitlinger, *The SS: Alibi of a Nation* (New York: Da Capo, 1957); Daniel Jonah Goldhagen, *Hitler's Willing Executioners: Ordinary Germans and the Holocaust* (New York: Vintage Books, 1996).

14. John Toland, *The Rising Sun: The Decline and Fall of the Japanese Empire* (New York: A Bantam Book, 1970), 759, 762.

15. Rhodes, *Atomic Bomb,* 586.

16. Richard Rhodes, *Dark Sun: The Making of the Hydrogen Bomb* (New York: Simon and Schuster, 1995), 21.

17. James Jones, *The Thin Red Line* (New York: Charles Scribner's Sons, 1962).

18. Eugene Sledge, *With the Old Breed: At Peleliu and Okinawa* (New York: Oxford University Press, 1981).

19. Paul Boyer, *By the Bomb's Early Light: American Thought and Culture at the Dawn of the Atomic Age* (New York: Pantheon Books, 1985), 226.

20. Fyodor Dostoyevsky, *The Brothers Karamazov* (New York: Grosset & Dunlap, n.d.), 266.

21. Ernest Hemingway, *A Farewell to Arms* (New York: Modern Library, 1932), 196.

22. Victor Davis Hanson, *An Autumn of War: What America Learned From September 11 and the War on Terrorism* (New York: Anchor Books, 2002), 32, 104.

23. Dostoyevsky, *The Brothers Karamazov*, 269.

Chapter 2

1. J. Glenn Gray, *The Warriors: Reflections on Men in Battle* (New York: Perennial Library, 1973), 60–61.
2. Bill Mauldin, *Up Front* (New York: W. W. Norton, 1968), 14.
3. S. L. A. Marshall, *Men Against Fire: The Problem of Battle Command in Future War* (Toronto: George J. McLeod, Ltd., 1947), 56–57. For other serious interpretations of the moral dilemma of the combat infantryman, *see* Joanna Bourke, *An Intimate History of Killing* (New York: Basic Books, 1999) and Lt. Col. Dave Grossman, *On Killing* (Boston: Little, Brown and Company, 1996).
4. Fredric Smoler, "The Secret of the Soldiers Who Didn't Shoot," *American Heritage Magazine* 40 (March 1989): 36–45.
5. Harold Leinbaugh and John D. Campbell, *The Men of Company K: The Autobiography of a World War II Rifle Company* (New York: William Morrow and Company, 1985).
6. John C. McManus, *The Deadly Brotherhood: The American Combat Soldier in World War II* (Novato, CA: Presidio Press, 1998), 99.
7. Smoler, "The Secret of Soldiers," 45.
8. Marshall, *Men Against Fire*, 79.
9. Herbert L. Abrams, "The Shadow of Accidental Nuclear War: The Irreparable Evil," in *Facing Evil: Confronting the Dreadful Power Behind Genocide, Terrorism, and Cruelty*, eds. Paul Woodruff and Harry A. Wilmer (Chicago and La Salle, IL: Open Court, 1988), 168.
10. Thomas Merton, *Ways of the Christian Mystics: Essays From Mystics and Zen Masters* (Boston: Shambhala Publications, 1993), 24.
11. Richard Maxwell Brown, *No Duty to Retreat* (New York: Oxford University Press, 1991), 3–5.
12. Page Smith, *A New Age Now Begins,* vol. 1 (New York: McGraw-Hill, 1976), 127.

13. William H. Nelson and Frank E. Vandiver, *Fields of Glory* (New York: E. P. Dutton & Company, 1960), 127; Russell F. Weigley, *Eisenhower's Lieutenants* (Bloomington: Indiana University Press, 1981), 2–7.
14. Brown, *No Duty*, chap. 1.
15. Rick Atkinson, *An Army at Dawn: The War in North Africa, 1942–1943* (New York: Henry Holt and Company, 2002), 261, 461–63; Donald V. Bennett and William R. Forstchen, *Honor Untarnished: A West Point Graduate's Memoir of World War II* (New York: A Tom Doherty Associates Book, 2003), 117.
16. Quoted in Weigley, *Eisenhower's Lieutenants*, 7.
17. Philip Caputo, *A Rumor of War* (New York: Ballantine Books, 1977), 129.
18. Robert D. Putnam, *Bowling Alone: The Collapse and Revival of American Community* (New York: Simon and Schuster, 2000).
19. *Statistical Abstract of the United States, 2004–2005* (Washington, D.C.: U.S. Bureau of the Census), 88.
20. *World Almanac, 2005*, 75.
21. Bart Farkas, *Call of Duty: Finest Hour* (Indianapolis: Activision, 2004).
22. Steven Lee Myers, "Haunting Thoughts After a Fierce Battle," *New York Times*, March 28, 2003.
23. Bob Herbert, "The Pain Deep Inside," *New York Times*, August 8, 2005.
24. Thomas Wortham, James Russell Lowell's *The Biglow Papers [First Series]: A Critical Edition* (DeKalb: Northern Illinois University Press, 1977), 51.

Chapter 3

1. Siegfried Sassoon, *Collected Poems, 1908–1956* (London: Faber and Faber, 1984), 86–87.
2. Tom Mathews, *Our Father's War: Growing Up in the Shadow of the Greatest Generation* (New York: Broadway Books, 2005), 226.
3. Bob Reed, personal communication, fall 2003 and winter 2004.

4. Personal experience and papers. I was a member of the Army Specialized Training Program, August 1943–March 1944.

Chapter 4

1. John Keegan, *The Face of Battle* (New York: Viking Press, 1976), 77.
2. Jones, *The Thin Red Line*, 172, 276, 295.
3. Charles Whiting, *America's Forgotten Army: The True Story of the U.S. Seventh Army in WWII—And An Unknown Battle That Changed History* (New York: St. Martin's Paperbacks, 1999), 150–51.
4. Michael Doubler, *Closing With the Enemy* (Lawrence: University of Kansas Press, 1994), 242.
5. Paul Fussell, *Wartime* (New York: Oxford University Press, 1989), 281.
6. Gerald F. Linderman, *The World Within War: America's Combat Experience in World War II* (New York: Free Press, 1997), 356.
7. Michael C. C. Adams, *The Best War Ever: America and World War II* (Baltimore, MD: John Hopkins University Press, 1994); Charles Whiting, *'44: In Combat From Normandy to the Ardennes* (New York: Cooper Square Press Edition, 2002); Paul Fussell, *Doing Battle: The Making of a Skeptic* (Boston: Little, Brown and Co., 1996); Linderman, *The World Within War*; Fussell, *Wartime*; Jones, *The Thin Red Line*; Mack Morris, "My Old Outfit," in *Yank, The Story of World War II as Written by Its Soldiers* (New York: Greenwich House, 1984), 259.
8. Fussell, *Wartime*, 268.
9. Stephen Ambrose, *Citizen Soldiers: The U.S. Army From the Normandy Beaches to the Bulge to the Surrender of Germany* (New York: Simon and Schuster, 1997), 472.
10. Tom Brokaw, *The Greatest Generation* (New York: Random House, 1998), xx.
11. "Rising U.S. and Chinese Oil Dependence: Time for Cooperation, not Confrontation," (Washington, DC: FCNL, July/August, 2005).

12. Richard Rubin, "Ghosts of Emmet Till," *New York Times Magazine*, July 31, 2005.
13. Gerald F. Linderman, *Embattled Courage: The Experience of Combat in the Civil War* (New York: Free Press, 1987), epilogue.
14. Siegfried Sassoon, *Collected Poems, 1908–1956* (London: Faber and Faber, 1984), 86–87.

Chapter 5

1. Edward W. Wood, Jr., *On Being Wounded* (Golden, CO: Fulcrum Publishing, 1991).
2. Fyodor Dostoyevsky, *Notes From the Underground*, trans. Mirra Ginsberg (New York: Bantam Books, 1974), 44–45.
3. Fussell, *Doing Battle*; Eugene Sledge, *With the Old Breed*; William Manchester, *Goodbye, Darkness: A Memoir of the Pacific War* (New York: Dell Publishing, 1979); Raymond Gantter, *Roll Me Over: An Infantryman's World War II* (New York: Ballantine Books, 1997); J. Glenn Gray, *The Warriors: Reflections on Men in Battle* (New York: Perennial Library, 1973), 60, 61; Howard Zinn, *Howard Zinn on War* (New York: Seven Stories Press, 2001), 105–20.
4. Jean Moulin, *Premier Combat* (Paris: Les Éditions de Minuit, 1983).
5. Ted Morgan, *An Uncertain Hour: The French, the Germans, the Jews, the Klaus Barbie Trial and the City of Lyon, 1940–1945* (London: The Bodley Head, 1990).
6. Wilfred Owen, *The Collected Poems of Wilfred Owen*, ed. C. Day Lewis (New York: New Directions, 1965), 55.
7. Paul Fussell, *Wartime: Understanding and Behavior in the Second World War* (New York: Oxford University Press, 1989; Fussell, *Doing Battle*; Fussell, *The Great War and Modern Memory* (Oxford: Oxford University Press, 1977); Zinn, *Zinn on War*; Zinn, *A People's History of the United States* (New York: Harper and Row, 1980); Samuel Hynes, *The Soldiers' Tale: Bearing Witness to Modern War* (New York: Penguin, 1997); Gerald F. Linderman, *Embattled*

Courage: The Experience of Combat in the Civil War
(New York: Free Press, 1987); Linderman, *The World
Within War*, 1997; Richard Holmes, *Acts of War: The
Behavior of Men in Battle* (New York: Free Press,
1985); Patrick K. O'Donnell, *Beyond Valor: World
War II's Rangers and Airborne Veterans Reveal the
Heart of Combat* (New York: Touchstone Press,
2001).
8. George L. Mosse, *Fallen Soldiers: Reshaping the
Memory of the World Wars* (New York: Oxford
University Press, 1990), 181.
9. Mosse, *Fallen Soldiers.*

Chapter 6

1. Peter R. Mansoor, *The GI Offensive in Europe: The
Triumph of American Infantry Divisions, 1941–1945*
(Lawrence: University Press of Kansas, 1999), 40–
43.
2. Cooney and Michalowski, *The Power of the People*,
53.
3. Norman Mailer, *The Naked and the Dead* (New York:
Rinehart and Company, 1948), 85, 322.

Chapter 7

1. Harry S. Ashmore, *Unseasonable Truths: The Life of
Robert Maynard Hutchins* (Boston: Little, Brown and
Co., 1989), 260–61.
2. Ashmore, *Unseasonable Truths*, 263.
3. Boyer, *Bomb's Early Light*, 123–24.
4. Boyer, *Bomb's Early Light*, 53.
5. Boyer, *Bomb's Early Light*, 54–56.
6. MacMillan, *Paris 1919*, 71, 75; Carlo D'Este, *Patton:
A Genius for War* (New York: Harper Perennial,
1995), 763.
7. David Irving, trans., *The Service: The Memoirs of
General Reinhard Gehlen* (New York: World
Publishing, 1972).
8. Albert Fried, ed., *McCarthyism: The Great American
Red Scare* (New York: Oxford University Press,
1997); Ellen Schrecker, *Many Are the Crimes:
McCarthyism in America* (Boston: Little, Brown, and

Co., 1998), 58, 59; David Caute, *The Great Fear: The Anti-Communist Purge Under Truman and Eisenhower* (New York: Simon and Schuster, 1978), 20.

9. Irving, *The Service.*

10. Joseph C. Goulden, *The Best Years: 1945–1950* (New York: Atheneum, 1976), 307.

11. Caute, *The Great Fear*, 283.

12. Staughton Lynd, "The Cold War Expulsions and the Movement of the 1960s," *Labor Solidarity Pamphlet*, no. 1, 1999.

13. Taylor Branch, *Pillar of Fire: America in the King Years, 1963–1965* (New York: Simon and Schuster, 1998), 114–15.

14. Adam Cohen and Elizabeth Taylor, *American Pharaoh: Mayor Richard Daley, His Battle for Chicago and the Nation* (Boston: Little, Brown and Co., 2001), 109–110.

15. Ed Holmgren, personal communication with the author, November 24, 2005.

16. Peter Beinart, "A Fighting Faith," *New Republic* 231 (December 13, 2004): 17.

17. James Weinstein, *The Long Detour* (Boulder, CO: Westview Press, 2003).

18. Nina Burleigh, *A Very Private Woman: The Life and Unsolved Murder of Presidential Mistress Mary Meyer* (New York: Bantam Books, 1998); Cord Meyer, Jr., *Facing Reality* (New York: Harper and Row, 1980).

19. Linderman, *The World Within War*, 1.

Chapter 8

1. Christopher Cooper and Alan Cullison, "Bush, Putin Steer Past Hot Topics, Stress Interests: Aides to Both Leaders Say U.S. President's Rebuke Doesn't Damage Relations," *Wall Street Journal*, May 9, 2005.

2. Murray and Millett, *A War To Be Won*, 282–91, 294–98.

3. Toland, *The Rising Sun*, 694.

4. Page Smith, *A New Age Now Begins*, vol. 1 (New York: McGraw-Hill, 1976), 132.

5. Richard Drinnon, *Facing West: The Metaphysics of Indian-Hating and Empire Building* (New York: Meridian, 1980).

6. Geoffrey Perret, *A Country Made by War: From the Revolution to Vietnam—The Story of America's Rise to Power* (New York: Random House, 1989); T. Harry Williams, *The History of American Wars: From Colonial Times to World War I* (New York: Alfred A. Knopf, 1981); Robert Leckie, *The Wars of America* (Edison, NJ: Castle Books, 1998); Halberstam, *War in a Time of Peace*; Clyde Prestowitz, *Rogue Nation* (New York: Basic Books, 2003); Phillip Berryman, *Stubborn Hope: Religion, Politics, and Revolution in Central America* (Maryknoll, NY: Orbis Books; New York: The New Press, 1994); Peter Kornbluh, *The Pinochet File* (New York: The New Press, 2003); David Halberstam, *The Fifties* (New York: Villard Books, 1993): William Blum, *Killing Hope* (Monroe, ME: Common Courage Press, 2004).

7. Richard Overy, *Why the Allies Won* (New York: W. W. Norton, 1995).

8. Henry Nash Smith, *Virgin Land: The American West as Symbol and Myth* (New York: Vintage Books, 1950), 64–76.

9. James Webb, *Born Fighting: How the Scots-Irish Shaped America* (New York: Broadway Books, 2004).

10. Overy, *Why the Allies Won*, 331–32.

11. Murray and Millett, *A War to Be Won*, 558; John Keegan, *The Second World War* , 591; Hook, *Third Reich*, 232; Saari and Saari, eds., *The Holocaust and World War II Almanac*, 2:381–83.

12. Murray and Millett, *A War to Be Won*, 554–58; Keegan, *The Second World War*, 590–91; Hook, *Third Reich*, 232; Saari and Saari, *Holocaust*, 381–83; Catherine Merridale, *A Night of Stone: Death and Memory in Twentieth Century Russia* (New York: Viking Penguin, 2000), 215–16.

13. Richard A. Clarke, *Against All Enemies: Inside America's War on Terror* (New York: Free Press, 2004), 24.

Chapter 9

1. For a copy of this photograph see Barbara Tuchman, *Stillwell and the American Experience in China* (New York: MacMillan, 1971), among the photographs following page 174.
2. Gorton Carruth, Jr., *The Encyclopedia of World Facts and Dates* (New York: Harper Collins, 1993), 653, 673, 677, 682, 663–95.
3. Jan Valtin, *Out of the Night* (New York: Alliance Book Corporation, 1941), 549–50.
4. Distel and Jakusch, *Concentration Camp Dachau*.
5. Howard Zinn, "The Scourge of Nationalism," *Progressive* 69 (June 2005): 12–13.
6. A reproduction of the photo is printed in Distel and Jakusch, *Concentration Camp Dachau*, 75.
7. Jane Mayer, "A Deadly Interrogation," *New Yorker*, November 14, 2005, 44–51.
8. Maureen Dowd, "Torture Chicks Gone Wild," *New York Times*, January 30, 2005.
9. Wortham, James Russell Lowell's *The Biglow Papers*, 62.
10. Carruth, *World Facts*, 672–73, 676, 686.
11. MacMillan, *Paris, 1919*, 377–409.
12. Alexander Cockburn, "Bombs, the Moral Tools of the West," *Los Angeles Times*, February 3, 1991.
13. Jeffery Goldberg, "Breaking Ranks," *New Yorker*, October 31, 2005, 56.
14. Many of the books in the bibliography have helped me gain the historical perspective described in this chapter. But I found the following books to be especially helpful: Elmer Bendiner, *A Time of Angels* (New York: Alfred A. Knopf, 1975); Piers Brendon, *The Dark Valley: A Panorama of the 1930's* (New York: Alfred A. Knopf, 2000); Huntington Gilchrist, *Imperialism and the Mandate System* (New York: League of Nations Non-Partisan Association, 1927); Alistair Horne, *The Price of Glory: Verdun 1916* (New York: Penguin, 1962); John E. Mack, *A Prince of Our Disorder: The Life of T. E. Lawrence* (Boston: Little, Brown and Co., 1976); Margaret MacMillan, *Paris*

1919 (New York: Random House, 2003); George L. Mosse, *Fallen Soldiers: Reshaping the Memory of the World Wars* (New York: Oxford University Press, 1990).

Chapter 10

1. Zinn, *Zinn on War*, 50.
2. *Statistical Abstract of the United States, 2004–2005* (Washington, D.C.: U.S. Bureau of the Census), 332.
3. *World Almanac, 2005*, 227; *Statistical Abstract*, 333; Huchthausen, *America's Splendid Little Wars*.
4. Thom Shanker, "U.S. Remains Leader in Global Arms Sales, Report Says," *New York Times*, September 25, 2003.
5. Howard Zinn, *Just War* (Milan: Edizioni Charta, 2005), 54.
6. Laurence Critchell, "The Distant Drum Is Still," in *Combat*, ed. Don Congdon (New York: Dell Publishing, 1963), 384.
7. Ernest Hemingway, *For Whom the Bell Tolls* (London: Grafton Books, 1989), 177–79.
8. Paul Fussell, *Wartime* (New York: Oxford University Press, 1989), 268.
9. Bob Baron, ed., *The Soul of America*, vol. 1 (Golden, CO: North American Press, 1994), 19; Joseph J. Ellis, *Founding Brothers: The Revolutionary Generation* (New York: Alfred A. Knopf, 2000), 81–119; John Woolman, *The Journal of John Woolman* (Secaucus, NJ: The Citadel Press, 1972).
10. Henry Mayer, *All on Fire: William Lloyd Garrison and the Abolition of Slavery* (New York: St. Martin's Griffin, 1998), frontispiece.
11. Putnam, *Bowling Alone*, 367–401, 404.
12. *Peaceful Prevention of Deadly Conflict* (Washington, D.C.: Friends Committee on National Legislation, 2004), 2–3.
13. Norman Podhoretz, "World War IV: How It Started; What It Means; and Why We Have to Win," in *Commentary*, September 2004, available at www.commentarymagazine.com; Robert D. Kaplan, "How We Would Fight China," *Atlantic Monthly*

Volume 295 (June 2005): 49–64; David E. Sanger, "Why Not a Strike on Iran?" *New York Times*, January 22, 2006.

14. John Ferling, *A Leap in the Dark: The Struggle to Create the American Republic* (New York: Oxford University Press, 2003).

Permissions

Excerpts from "The Biglow Papers," by James Russell Lowell, by kind permission of Northern Illinois University Press, *The Biglow Papers [First Series] A Critical Edition*, edition by Thomas Wortham. © 1977, DeKalb: Northern Illinois University Press.

"Dulce et Decorum Est," by Wilfred Owen, from *The Collected Poems of Wilfred Owen* © 1963 by Chatto & Windus, Ltd. Reprinted by permission of New Directions Publishing Corp.

"Song-Books of the War," from *Collected Poems of Siegfried Sassoon* by Siegfried Sassoon. © 1918, 1920 by E. P. Dutton. © 1936, 1946, 1947, 1948 by Siegfried Sassoon. Copyright Siegfried Sassoon by kind permission of the Estate of George Sassoon. Used by permission of Viking Penguin, a division of Penguin Group (USA) Inc.

Chapter 4 is based on the revision of a commentary, "On Judging World War Two: The Greatest Generation," which appeared in *War, Literature & the Arts, an International Journal of the Humanities*, (Fall-Winter 2000), Department of English and Fine Arts, United States Air Force Academy, Colorado Springs, Colorado. The author extends his thanks to the editor and the staff for the use of this material.

And a kind thank you to Lori Grinker
for her photograph of the author.

~~~

SELECTED BIBLIOGRAPHY

The following books are but a small sample of books that I read as I struggled to reach the understandings of World War II reflected in this book. I well remember when that search for understanding first became conscious. I had been troubled for years, been through a difficult divorce, often changed jobs, was pursued by a general malaise. I had no understanding that the causes for my difficulties were rooted in World War II and my experience of it. Still a city planner, I lived on Cape Cod, working for an environmental planning firm there. On a consulting assignment in Washington, D.C., in 1978 or 1979, I browsed through a bookstore one evening. By chance I picked up a remaindered copy of Anthony Cave Brown's *Bodyguard of Lies*.

That book seized my imagination. I devoured it over dinner, late into the night, and the next day, reading it whenever I could. It opened me to memories long repressed: the war, what I had done in it, the fact of being wounded, my fears, my shame. I remember being shaken as I read it, even crying. It was as though I had been swimming underwater for years and suddenly had popped into the bright light of memory. When I finished the book two days later, my life began to change, never to be the same again. On the deepest level of my being, I realized I had to understand that war and what it had done to me and my generation.

That book led to reading another and another and another. Those books convinced me to return to France. That voyage into the past began my writing. Three published books later, I still struggle with the meaning of that war and hope, if I live long enough, to add another finished book to this list.

So this bibliography is not just a dry recording of books I read to satisfy some academic require-ment or intellectual pursuit. They are the lifeblood of my being. I sit now, surrounded by them, on shelves, on desks, on floors. Each time I bring more into the house, Elaine shakes her head. But these books tell the story of over a quarter of a century of searching for the meaning of war in America.

As I end this book, I must thank their authors for their contribution to my life. I owe so much to them, only a few of whom are listed below. Without their work, I never would have reached this under-standing of war and World War II, an understanding that has saved my life.

Abrams, Herbert L. "The Shadow of Accidental Nuclear War: The Irreparable Evil." In *Facing Evil: Confronting the Dreadful Power Behind Genocide, Terrorism, and Cruelty,* edited by Paul Woodruff and Harry A. Wilmer. Chicago and La Salle, IL: Open Court Publishing, 1988.

Adams, Michael C. C. *The Best War Ever: America and World War II*. Baltimore, MD: Johns Hopkins University Press, 1994.

Alexander, Bevin. *How America Got It Right: The U.S. March to Military and Political Supremacy*. New York: Crown Forum, 2005.

Ambrose, Stephen. *Band of Brothers: E Company, 506th Regiment, 101st Airborne from Normandy to Hitler's Eagle Nest*. New York: Touchstone, 1992.

———. *Citizen Soldiers: The U.S. Army From the Normandy Beaches to the Bulge to the Surrender of Germany*. New York: Simon and Schuster, 1997.

———. *D-Day: June 6, 1944, The Climatic Battle of World War II*. New York: Simon and Schuster, 1994.

———. *The Victors: Eisenhower and His Boys: The Men of World War II*. New York: Simon and Schuster, 1998.

Anderson, Donald, ed. *Aftermath: An Anthology of Post-Vietnam Fiction*. New York: Henry Holt, 1995.

Anderson, Fred, and Andrew Cayton. *The Dominion of War: Empire and Liberty in America, 1500–2000*. New York: Viking, 2005.

Arendt, Hannah. *On Violence*. New York: Harvest Books, 1970.

Ashmore, Harry S. *Unseasonable Truths: The Life of Robert Maynard Hutchins*. Boston: Little, Brown, and Co., 1989.

Atkinson, Rick. *An Army at Dawn: The War in North Africa, 1942–1943*. New York: Henry Holt, 2002.

———. *The Long Gray Line: The American Journey of West Point's Class of 1966*. New York: Henry Holt, 1989.

Baron, Robert C., ed. *Soul of America: Documenting Our Past. Vol. I, 1492–1870*. Golden, CO: North American Press, 1994.

Bates, H. E. *Fair Stood the Wind for France*. Boston: Little, Brown, and Co., 1944.

Beck, Earl R. *Under the Bombs: The German Home Front, 1942–1945*. Lexington: University Press of Kentucky, 1986.

Becker, Ernest. *The Denial of Death*. New York: Free Press, 1973.

———. *Escape From Evil*. New York: Free Press, 1975.

Bendiner, Elmer. *A Time for Angels: The Tragicomic History of the League of Nations*. New York: Alfred A. Knopf, 1975.

Bennett, Donald V., and William R. Forstchen. *Honor Untarnished: A West Point Graduate's Memoir of World War II*. New York: Tom Doherty Associates, 2003.

Bennett, Michael J. *When Dreams Came True: The GI Bill and the Making of America*. Washington, D.C.: Brassey's, Inc., 1996.

Berryman, Phillip. *Stubborn Hope: Religion, Politics, and Revolution in Central America*. Maryknoll, NY: Orbis Books, 1984.

Blum, John Morton. *V Was for Victory*. New York: Harvest Books, 1976.

Blum, William. *Killing Hope: U.S. Military and CIA Interventions Since World War II*. Monroe, ME: Common Courage Press, 2004.

Blunt, Roscoe C., Jr. *Foot Soldier: A Combat Infantryman's War in Europe*. New York: Da Capo Press, 2001.

Bok, Sissela. *Mayhem*. Reading, MA: Addison Wesley, 1998.

Boot, Max. *The Savage Wars of Peace: Small Wars and the Rise of American Power*. New York: Basic Books, 2002.

Boritt, Gabor S., ed. *War Comes Again: Comparative Vistas on the Civil War and World War II*. New York: Oxford University Press, 1995.

Bourke, Joanna. *An Intimate History of Killing: Face-to-Face Killing in 21st Century Warfare*. New York: Basic Books, 1999.

Bowden, Mark. *Blackhawk Down: A Story of Modern War*. New York: Atlantic Monthly Press, 1999.

Bowen, Robert. *The Weight of the Cross*. New York: Alfred Knopf, 1951.

Boyer, Paul. *By the Bomb's Early Light: American Thought and Culture at the Dawn of the Atomic Age*. New York: Pantheon Books, 1985.

Bradley, James, with Ron Powers. *Flags of Our Fathers*. New York: Bantam Books, 2000.

Branch, Taylor. *Pillar of Fire: America in the King Years 1963–1965*. New York: Simon and Schuster, 1988.

Brendon, Piers. *The Dark Valley: A Panorama of the 1930s*. New York: Alfred A. Knopf, 2000.

Brokaw, Tom. *An Album of Memories: Personal Histories From the Greatest Generation*. New York: Random House, 2001.

———. *The Greatest Generation*. New York: Random House, 1998.

———. *The Greatest Generation Speaks: Letters and Reflections*. New York: Random House, 1999.

Brown, Anthony Cave. *Bodyguard of Lies: The Extraordinary, True Story of the Clandestine War of Deception That Hid the Secrets of D-Day From Hitler and Sealed the Allied Victory*. New York: Bantam Books, 1978.

Brown, Richard Maxwell. *No Duty to Retreat: Violence and Values in American History and Culture*. New York: Oxford University Press, 1991.

Browning, Christopher R. *Ordinary Men: Reserve Battalion 101 and the Final Solution in Poland*. New York: Harper Perennial, 1992.

Burleigh, Nina. *A Very Private Woman: The Life and Unsolved Murder of Presidential Mistress Mary Meyer*. New York: Bantam Books, 1998.

Caputo, Philip. *A Rumor of War*. New York: Ballantine Books, 1977.

Carruth, Gorton, Jr. *The Encyclopedia of American Facts and Dates*. New York: Harper Collins, 1997.

———. *The Encyclopedia of World Facts and Dates*. New York: Harper Collins, 1993.

Caute, David. *The Great Fear: The Anti-Communist Purge Under Truman and Eisenhower*. New York: Simon and Schuster, 1978.

Chang, Iris. *The Rape of Nanking: The Forgotten Holocaust of World War II*. New York: Penguin, 1997.

Clarke, Richard A. *Against All Enemies: Inside America's War on Terror*. New York: Free Press, 2004.

Cohen, Adam, and Elizabeth Taylor. *American Pharaoh: Mayor Richard Daley, His Battle for Chicago and the Nation*. Boston: Little, Brown, and Co., 2001.

Cooney, Robert, and Helen Michalowski. *The Power of the People: Active Nonviolence in the United States*. Culver City, CA: Peace Press, 1977.

Critchell, Laurence. "The Distant Drum Was Still," in
      Combat, ed. Don Cougdon. New York: Dell
      Publishing, 1963.

Cornwell, John. *Hitler's Pope: The Secret History of Pius
      XII*. New York: Viking, 1999.

cummings, e. e. *The Enormous Room*. New York:
      Liveright Publications, 1978.

Dawidowicz, Lucy S. *The War Against the Jews: 1933–
      1945*. New York: Holt, Rinehart and Winston, 1975.

Dear, I. C. B., ed. *The Oxford Companion to World War II*.
      Oxford: Oxford University Press, 1995.

D'Este, Carlo. *Patton: A Genius for War*. New York:
      Harper Perennial, 1995.

Distel, Barbara, and Ruth Jakusch, eds. *Concentration
      Camp Dachau, 1933–1945*. Translated by Jennifer
      Vernon. Brussels: Comité International de Dachau,
      1978.

Dostoyevsky, Fydor. *Notes From the Underground*.
      Translated by Mirra Ginsberg. New York: Bantam
      Books, 1974.

———. *The Brothers Karamazov*. New York: Grosset and
      Dunlap, n.d.

Doubler, Michael. *Closing With the Enemy: How GI's
      Fought the War in Europe, 1944–1945*. Lawrence:
      University of Kansas Press, 1994.

Drinnon, Richard. *Facing West: The Metaphysics of
      Indian-Hating and Empire Building*. New York:
      Meridian Books, 1980.

Ehrenreich, Barbara. *Blood Rites: Origins and History of
      the Passions of War*. New York: Metropolitan Books,
      1997.

Ellis, Joseph J. *Founding Brothers: The Revolutionary
      Generation*. New York: Alfred A. Knopf, 2000.

Feig, Konnilyn G. *Hitler's Death Camps: The Sanity of
      Madness*. New York: Holmes and Meier Publishers,
      1979.

Ferguson, Niall. *Colossus: The Price of America's Empire*.
      New York: Penguin, 2004.

Ferling, John. *A Leap in the Dark: The Struggle to Create
      the American Republic*. New York: Oxford University
      Press, 2003.

Fest, Joachim C. *The Face of the Third Reich: Portrait of the Nazi Leadership*. Translated by Michael Bullock. New York: Pantheon Books, 1970.

Field, Hermann, and Stanislaw Mierzenski. *Angry Harvest*. New York: Thomas Y. Crowell, 1958.

Foster, Kevin. *Fighting Fictions: War, Narrative and National Identity*. London: Pluto Press, 1999.

Fried, Albert. *McCarthyism: The Great American Red Scare, A Documentary History*. New York: Oxford University Press, 1997.

Friedrich, Ernst. *War Against War*. Seattle: The Real Comet Press, 1987.

Friends Committee on National Legislation. *Peaceful Prevention of Deadly Conflict*. Washington, D.C., 2004.

Fussell, Paul. *The Great War and Modern Memory*. Oxford: Oxford University Press, 1977.

———. *Doing Battle: The Making of a Skeptic*. Boston, MA: Little, Brown, 1996.

———. *Wartime: Understanding and Behavior in the Second World War*. New York: Oxford University Press, 1989.

Gajdusek, Robert E. *Resurrection: A War Journey*. Notre Dame, IN: Notre Dame Press, 1997.

Galloway, K. Bruce, and Robert Bowie Johnson, Jr. *West Point: America's Power Fraternity*. New York: Simon and Schuster, 1973.

Gantter, Raymond. *Roll Me Over: An Infantryman's World War II*. New York: Ballantine Books, 1997.

Gellhorn, Martha. *The Face of War*. New York: Atlantic Monthly Press, 1988.

Gilchrist, Huntington. *Imperialism and the Mandate System*. New York: The League of Nations Non-Partisan Association, 1927.

Gildea, Robert. *Marianne in Chains: Daily Life in the Heart of France During the German Occupation*. New York: Metropolitan Books, 2002.

Goldhagen, Daniel Jonah. *Hitler's Willing Executioners: Ordinary Germans and the Holocaust*. New York: Vintage Books, 1996.

Goldston, Robert. *The Road Between the Wars: 1918–1941*. New York: Fawcett Crest, 1978.

Goulden, Joseph C. *The Best Years: 1945–1950*. New York: Atheneum, 1976.

Gray, J. Glenn. *The Warriors: Reflections on Men in Battle*. New York: Perennial Library, 1973.

Green, Martin. *Tolstoy and Gandhi, Men of Peace: A Biography*. New York: Basic Books, 1983.

Grinker, Lori. *Afterwar: Veterans From a World in Conflict*. Millbrook, NY: de.MO, 2004.

Grossman, Dave. *On Killing: The Psychological Cost of Learning to Kill in War and Society*. Boston: Little, Brown, and Co., 1996.

Halberstam, David. *The Fifties*. New York: Villard Books, 1993.

———. *War in a Time of Peace: Bush, Clinton, and the Generals*. New York: Scribner, 2001.

Hallie, Philip. *Lest Innocent Blood Be Shed: The Story of the Village of Le Chambon and How Goodness Happened There*. New York: Harper Colophon Books, 1979.

Halpert, Sam. *A Real Good War*. St. Petersburg, FL: Southern Heritage Press, 1997.

Hanley, Charles J., Sang-Hun Choe, and Martha Mendoza. *The Bridge at No Gun Ri: A Hidden Nightmare From the Korean War*. New York: Henry Holt, 2001.

Hanson, Victor Davis. *An Autumn of War: What America Learned From September 11 and the War on Terrorism*. New York: Anchor Books, 2002.

———. *Carnage and Culture: Landmark Battles in the Rise of Western Power*. New York: Doubleday, 2001.

———. *Ripples of Battle: How Wars of the Past Still Determine How We Fight, How We Live, and How We Think*. New York: Doubleday, 2003.

———. *The Soul of Battle: From Ancient Times to the Present Day, How Three Great Liberators Vanquished Tyranny*. New York: Free Press, 1999.

Hastings, Max. *Armageddon: The Battle for Germany, 1944–1945*. New York: Alfred A. Knopf, 2004.

Hedges, Chris. *War Is a Force That Gives Us Meaning*. New York: Public Affairs, 2002.

Heller, Joseph. *Catch 22*. New York: Scribner, 1961.

Hellman, Lillian. *Scoundrel Time*. Boston: Little, Brown and Co., 1976.

Hemingway, Ernest. *A Farewell to Arms*. New York: Modern Library, 1932.

———. *For Whom the Bell Tolls*. London: Grafton Books, 1989.

———. *The Sun Also Rises*. In *The Hemingway Reader*, ed. Charles Poore. New York: Charles Scribner's Sons, 1927–1966.

Hersh, Burton. *The Old Boys: The American Elite and the Origins of the CIA*. St. Petersburg, FL: Tree Farm Books, 2002.

Hersey, John. *Hiroshima*. New York: Bantam Books, 1946.

Hillen, James. *Blue Helmets: The Strategy of UN Military Operations*. Washington, D.C.: Brassey's, Inc., 2000.

Hillman, James. *A Terrible Love of War*. New York: Penguin Press, 2004.

Holmes, Richard. *Acts of War: The Behavior of Men in Battle*. New York: Free Press, 1985.

Hook, Alex. *Illustrated History of the Third Reich*. Cobham, UK: TAJ Books, 2004.

Horne, Alistair. *The Price of Glory: Verdun 1916*. New York: Penguin Books, 1964.

Hoyt, Edwin P. *The GI's War: American Soldiers in Europe During World War II*. New York: Da Capo Press, 1988.

Hughes, Matthew, and Chris Mann. *Inside Hitler's Germany: Life in the Third Reich*. New York: MJF Books, 2000.

Huchthausen, Peter. *America's Splendid Little Wars: A Short History of U.S. Military Engagements: 1975–2000*. New York: Viking Penguin, 2003.

Huie, William Bradford. *Mud on the Stars*. New York: L. B. Fischer, 1942.

Hynes, Samuel. *The Soldiers' Tale: Bearing Witness to Modern War*. New York: Penguin, 1997.

Irving, David, trans. *The Service: The Memoirs of General Reinhard Gehlen*. New York: World Publishing, 1972.

Isenberg, Shelia. *A Hero of Our Own: The Story of Varian Fry*. New York: Random House, 2001.

James, Lawrence. *Warrior Race: A History of the British at War*. Reprint, Boston: Little, Brown, and Co., 2001.

Joffroy, Pierre. *A Spy for God: The Ordeal of Kurt Gerstein*. New York: The Universal Library, 1970.

Jones, James. *From Here To Eternity*. New York: Charles Scribner's Sons, 1951.

———. *The Pistol*. New York: A Dell Book, 1958.

———. *The Thin Red Line*. New York: Charles Scribner's Sons, 1962.

———. *Whistle*. New York: Delacorte Press, 1978.

Kagan, Donald. *On the Origins of War and the Preservation of Peace*. New York: Anchor Books, 1995.

———. *The Peloponnesian War*. New York: Penguin Books, 2004.

Kahn, E. J., Jr. *The China Hands: American Foreign Service Officers and What Befell Them*. New York: Viking Press, 1975.

Kaplan, Robert D. *Warrior Politics: Why Leadership Demands a Pagan Ethos*. New York: Random House, 2002.

Keegan, John. *The Face of Battle*. New York: Viking Press, 1976.

———. *The First World War*. New York: Vintage Books, 2000.

———. *The Second World War*. New York: Viking Press, 1989.

Kennedy, David M. *Over Here: The First World War and American Society*. New York: Oxford University Press, 1980.

Kennett, Lee. *GI: The American Soldier in World War II*. New York: Charles Scribner's Sons, 1987.

Kirschner, Allen, and Linda Kirschner, eds. *Blessed Are the Peacemakers*. New York: Popular Library, 1971.

Klee, Ernst, Willi Dressen, and Volker Riess, eds. Translated by Deborah Burnstone. *The Good Old*

Days: The Holocaust as Seen by Its Perpetrators and Bystanders. New York: Konecky & Konecky, 1988.

Knightley, Phillip. *The First Casualty: From the Crimea to Vietnam: The War Correspondent as Hero, Propagandist, and Myth Maker*. New York: Harcourt Brace Jovanovich, 1975.

Koch, H. W. *The Hitler Youth: Origins and Development, 1922–1945*. New York: Cooper Square Press, 2000.

———. *In the Name of the Volk: Political Justice in Hitler's Germany*. New York: Barnes & Noble Books, 1997.

Koltowitz, Robert. *Before Their Time*. New York: Anchor Books, 1998.

Kornbluh, Peter. *The Pinochet File: A Declassified Dossier of Atrocity and Accountability*. New York: The New Press, 2004.

Lech, Raymond B. *Broken Soldiers*. Urbana and Chicago, IL: University of Illinois Press, 2000.

Leckie, Robert. *The Wars of America*. Edison, NJ: Castle Books, 1998.

Lee, Laurie. *A Moment of War: A Memoir of the Spanish Civil War*. New York: New Press, 1991.

Leinbaugh, Harold P., and John D. Campbell. *The Men of Company K: The Autobiography of a World War II Rifle Company*. New York: William Morrow, 1985.

Lewy, Guenter. *The Catholic Church and Nazi Germany*. New York: Da Capo Press, 2000.

Lifton, Robert Jay, and Eric Markusen. *The Genocidal Mentality: Nazi Holocaust and Nuclear Threat*. New York: Basic Books, 1990.

Linderman, Gerald F. *Embattled Courage: The Experience of Combat in the Civil War*. New York: Free Press, 1987.

———. *The World Within War: America's Combat Experience in World War II*. New York: Free Press, 1997.

Lindquist, Sven. *A History of Bombing*. New York: New Press, 2001.

Lynd, Staughton, ed. *Nonviolence in America: A Documentary History*. New York: Bobbs-Merrill, 1966.

Lutz, Catherine. *Homefront*. Boston: Beacon Press, 2001.

224   Selected Bibliography

Mack, John E. *A Prince of Our Disorder: The Life of T. E. Lawrence*. Boston: Little, Brown, and Co., 1976.

MacMillan, Margaret. *Paris 1919: Six Months That Changed the World*. New York: Random House, 2003.

Mailer, Norman. *The Naked and the Dead*. New York: Rinehart, 1948.

Malraux, Andre. *Man's Hope*. New York: Grove Press, 1966.

Manchester, William. *American Caesar: Douglas MacArthur, 1880–1964*. Boston: Little, Brown, and Co., 1978.

———. *Goodbye, Darkness: A Memoir of the Pacific War*. New York: Dell Publishing, 1979.

Mansoor, Peter R. *The GI Offensive in Europe: The Triumph of American Infantry Divisions, 1941–1945*. Lawrence: University Press of Kansas, 1999.

Marquand, John P. *So Little Time*. Boston: Little, Brown, and Co., 1943.

Marshall, S. L. A. *Men Against Fire: The Problem of Battle Command in Future War*. Toronto: George J. McLeod, 1947.

———. *World War I*. New York: Houghton Mifflin, 2001.

Mathews, Tom. *Our Father's War: Growing Up in the Shadow of the Greatest Generation*. New York: Broadway Books, 2005.

Mauldin, Bill. *Up Front*. New York: W. W. Norton, 1968.

Mayer, Henry. *All On Fire: William Lloyd Garrison and the Abolition of Slavery*. New York: St. Martin's Griffin, 1998.

McElvaine, Robert S. *The Great Depression: America, 1929–1941*. New York: Times Books, 1993.

McManus, John C. *The Deadly Brotherhood: The American Combat Soldier in World War II*. Novato, CA: Presidio Press, 1998.

McShane, Frank. *Into Eternity: The Life of James Jones, American Writer*. Boston: Houghton Mifflin, 1985.

Meredith, James H. *Understanding the Literature of World War II: A Student Casebook to Issues, Sources, and Historical Documents*. Westport, CT: Greenwood Press, 1999.

Merridale, Catherine. *Night of Stone: Death and Memory in Twentieth-Century Russia*. New York: Penguin Books, 2000.

Merton, Thomas. *Faith and Violence: Christian Teaching and Christian Practice*. Notre Dame, IN: University of Notre Dame Press, 1968.

———. *Ways of the Christian Mystics: Essays From Mystics and Zen Masters*. Boston: Shambhala Publications, 1993.

Meyer, Cord Jr. *Facing Reality: From World Federalism to the CIA*. New York: Harper and Row, 1980.

Monsarrat, Nicholas. *The Cruel Sea*. New York: Alfred A. Knopf, 1951.

Moors, Bob "Red." *My 40-Year War*. La Mesa, CA: Associated Creative Writers, 1985.

Morgan, Ted. *An Uncertain Hour: The French, the Germans, the Jews, the Klaus Barbie Trial and the City of Lyon, 1940–1945*. London: The Bodley Head, 1990.

Morris, Willie. *James Jones: A Friendship*. New York: Dell Publishing. 1978.

Mosley, Leonard. *Marshall: Hero of Our Times*. New York: Hearst Books, 1982.

Mosse, George L. *Fallen Soldiers: Reshaping the Memory of the World Wars*. New York: Oxford University Press, 1990.

Moulin, Jean. *Premier Combat*. Paris: Les Éditions de Minuit, 1983.

Murray, Williamson, and Allan R. Millett. *A War to Be Won: Fighting the Second World War*. Cambridge, MA: Harvard University Press, 2000.

Neillands, Robin. *The Bomber War: The Allied Air Offensive Against Germany*. New York: Barnes & Noble Books, 2005.

Nelson, William H., and Frank E. Vandiver. *Fields of Glory*. New York: E. P. Dutton, 1960.

Novick, Peter. *The Holocaust in American Life*. Boston: Houghton Mifflin, 1999.

Oates, Whitney J., and Eugene O'Neill, Jr. *The Complete Greek Drama*. 2 vols. New York: Random House. 1938.

O'Connell, Robert L. *Of Arms and Men: A History of War, Weapons and Aggression*. New York: Oxford University Press, 1989.

O'Donnell, Patrick K. *Beyond Valor: World War II's Rangers and Airborne Veterans Reveal the Heart of Combat*. New York: Touchstone Press, 2001.

Orwell, George. *Homage to Catalonia*. Boston: Beacon Press, 1952.

Owen, Wilfred. *The Collected Poems of Wilfred Owen*. Edited by C. Day Lewis. New York: New Directions Paperbook, 1965.

Overy, Richard. *Why The Allies Won*. New York: W. W. Norton, 1995.

Pennell, Joseph Stanley. *The History of Rome Hanks and Kindred Matters*. Sag Harbor, NY: Second Chance Press, 1982.

Perret, Geoffrey. *A Country Made by War: From the Revolution to Vietnam—The Story of America's Rise to Power*. New York: Random House, 1989.

———. *There's a War to Be Won: The United States Army in World War II*. New York: Random House, 1991.

Phillips, John, *The Second Happiest Day*. New York: Harper and Brothers, Publishers, 1953.

Phillips, Kevin. *The Cousin's War: Religion, Politics, and the Triumph of Anglo-America*. New York: Basic Books, 1999.

Polk, William R. *Understanding Iraq: The Whole Sweep of Iraqi History, from Genghis Khan's Mongols to the Ottoman Turks to the British Mandate to the American Occupation*. New York: Harper Collins, 2005.

Prashker, Ivan. *Duty, Honor, Vietnam: Twelve Men of West Point*. New York: William Morrow, 1988.

Prestowitz, Clyde. *Rogue Nation: American Unilateralism and the Failure of Good Intentions*. New York: Basic Books, 2003.

Priest, Dana. *The Mission: Waging War and Keeping Peace With America's Military*. New York: W. W. Norton, 2003.

Putnam, Robert D. *Bowling Alone: The Collapse and Revival of American Community*. New York: Simon and Schuster, 2000.

Pyle, Ernie. *Brave Men*. New York: Henry Holt, 1944.

Reitlinger, Gerald. *The SS: Alibi of a Nation, 1922–1945*. New York: Da Capo Press, [1989], c1957.

Remarque, Erich Marie. *All Quiet on the Western Front*. Translated by A. W. Wheen. New York: Heritage Press, 1969.

Rhodes, Richard. *Dark Sun: The Making of the Hydrogen Bomb*. New York: Simon and Schuster, 1995.

———. *The Making of the Atomic Bomb*. New York: Simon and Schuster, 1986.

Rose, Lisle A. *The Cold War Comes to Main Street: America in 1950*. Lawrence: University Press of Kansas, 1999.

Royster, Charles. *The Destructive War: William Tecumseh Sherman, Stonewall Jackson, and the Americans*. New York: Vintage Books, 1993.

Saari, Peggy, and Aaron Maurice Saari, eds. *The Holocaust and World War II Almanac*, vol. 2. Detroit: Gale Group, 2001.

Sassoon, Siegfried. *Collected Poems, 1908–1956*. London: Faber and Faber, 1984.

———. *The Complete Memoirs of George Sherston*. London: Faber and Faber, 1937.

Scheuer, Michael. *Imperial Hubris: Why the West Is Losing the War on Terror*. Washington, D.C.: Brassey's, Inc., 2004.

Schlesinger, Arthur M., Jr. *War and the American Presidency*. New York: W. W. Norton, 2004.

Schlesinger, Stephen C. *Act of Creation: The Founding of the United Nations*. Boulder, CO: Westview Press, 2003.

Schrecker, Ellen. *Many Are the Crimes: McCarthyism in America*. Boston: Little, Brown, and Co., 1998.

Schrijvers, Peter. *The Crash of Ruin: American Combat Soldiers in Europe During World War II*. New York: New York University Press, 1998.

Sebald, W. G. *On the Natural History of Destruction*. Translated by Anthea Bell. New York: Random House, 2003.

Sereny, Gitta. *Into That Darkness: An Examination of Conscience*. New York: Vintage Books, 1983.

Shacochis, Bob. *The Immaculate Invasion*. New York: Viking Press, 1999.

Shaw, Irwin. *The Young Lions*. New York: Modern Library, 1976.

Shay, Jonathan. *Achilles in Vietnam: Combat Trauma and the Undoing of Character*. New York: A Touchstone Book, 1995.

Sherry, Michael S. *In the Shadow of War: The United States since the 1930s*. New Haven, CT: Yale University Press, 1995.

Sherwin, Martin J. *A World Destroyed: The Atomic Bomb and the Grand Alliance*. New York: Vintage Books, 1977.

Shute, Nevil. *Pastoral*. New York: William Morrow, 1944.

Sledge, Eugene. *With the Old Breed: At Peleliu and Okinawa*. New York: Oxford University Press, 1981.

Slotkin, Richard. *Gunfighter Nation: The Myth of the Frontier in Twentieth-Century America*. New York: Harper Perennial, 1993.

Smith, Henry Nash. *Virgin Land: The American West as Symbol and Myth*. New York: Vintage Books, 1950.

Smith, Page. *A New Age Now Begins*, vol. 1. New York: McGraw-Hill, 1976.

Smoler, Fredric. "The Secret of the Soldiers Who Didn't Shoot." *American Heritage Magazine* 40 (1989): 36–45.

Snow, Donald M., and Dennis M. Drew. *From Lexington to Desert Storm: War and Politics in the American Experience*. Armonk, NY: M. E. Sharpe, 1994.

Speer, Albert. *Inside the Third Reich*. Translated by Richard and Clara Winston. New York: Avon Books, 1970.

———. *Spandau: The Secret Diaries*. Translated by Richard and Clara Winston. New York: Pocketbooks, 1977.

Stokesbury, James L. *A Short History of World War II*. New York: William Murrow, 1980.

Sydnor, Charles W., Jr. *Soldiers of Destruction: The SS Death's Head Division, 1933–1945*. Princeton, NJ: Princeton University Press, 1977.

Takaki, Ronald. *Double Victory: A Multicultural History of America in World War II*. Boston: Little, Brown, Co., 2000.

Terkel, Studs. *The Good War: An Oral History of World War II*. New York: The New Press, 1984.

Thomas, Gordon, and Max Morgan Witts. *Voyage of the Damned*. New York: Stein and Day, 1974.

Time-Life Books. *WWII: The Illustrated History of World War II*. Alexandria, VA: 1999.

Todorov, Tzuetan. *Facing the Extreme: Moral Life in the Concentration Camp*. Translated by Arthur Derner and Abigail Pollack. New York: Metropolitan, 1996.

Toland, John. *The Rising Sun: The Decline and Fall of the Japanese Empire*. New York: Bantam Books, 1970.

Tolstoy, Leo. *War and Peace*. Translated by Rosemary Edmonds. New York: Greenwich House, 1982.

Townsend, Peter. *Duel of Eagles*. New York: Simon and Schuster, 1971.

Tuchman, Barbara. *Stillwell and the American Experience in China*. New York: MacMillan, 1971.

———. *The Guns of August*. New York: MacMillan, 1962.

———. *The Proud Tower: A Portrait of the World Before the War: 1890–1914*. New York: Bantam Books, 1967.

Twain, Mark. *The War Prayer*. New York: Harper Colophon Books, 1951.

Valtin, Jan. *Out of the Night*. New York: Alliance Corporation, 1941.

Vonnegut, Kurt. *Slaughterhouse Five*. New York: Dell Publishing, 1969.

Walker, Peter. *Moral Choices: Memory, Desire, and Imagination in Nineteenth-Century American Abolition*. Baton Rouge: Louisiana State University Press, 1978.

Walzer, Michael. *Just and Unjust Wars: A Moral Argument With Historical Illustrations*. New York: Basic Books, 1977.

Waugh, John C. *The Class of 1846: From West Point to Appomattox: Stonewall Jackson, George McClellan and Their Brothers*. New York: Ballantine Books, 1994.

Webb, James. *Born Fighting: How the Scots-Irish Shaped America*. New York: Broadway Books, 2004.

Webster, Donovan. *Aftermath: The Remnants of War*. New York: Pantheon Books, 1996.

Weigley, Russell F. *Eisenhower's Lieutenants: The Campaign of France and Germany, 1944–1945*. Bloomington: Indiana University Press, 1981.

Weinberg, Arthur, and Lila Weinberg, eds. *Instead of Violence*. Boston: Beacon Press, 1963.

Weinstein, James. *The Long Detour: The History and Future of the American Left*. Boulder, CO: Westview Press, 2003.

Whiting, Charles. *America's Forgotten Army: The True Story of the U.S. Seventh Army in WWII—And an Unknown Battle That Changed History*. New York: St. Martin's Press, 1999.

———. *'44: In Combat From Normandy to the Ardennes*. New York: Cooper Square Press, 2002.

Williams, Michael, ed. *They Walked With God*. New York: Fawcett Publications, 1962.

Williams, T. Harry. *The History of American Wars: From Colonial Times to World War I*. New York: Alfred A. Knopf, 1981.

Winik, Jay. *April 1865: The Month That Saved America*. New York: Perennial, 2002.

Wolfe, Thomas. *You Can't Go Home Again*. New York: Perennial Library, 1968.

Woolman, John. *The Journal of John Woolman*. Secaucus, NJ: The Citadel Press, 1972.

Wortham, Thomas. *James Russell Lowell's "The Biglow Papers [First Series]": A Critical Edition*. DeKalb: Northern Illinois University Press, 1977.

Wyden, Peter. *The Passionate War: The Narrative History of the Spanish Civil War, 1936–1939*. New York: Simon and Schuster, 1983.

Zentner, Christian, and Friedemann Bedürftig, eds. English translation edited by Amy Hackett. *The Encyclopedia of the Third Reich*, vol. 2. New York: Macmillan Publishing, 1991.

Zinn, Howard. *Howard Zinn on War*. New York: Seven
  Stories Press, 2001.
———. *A People's History of the United States*. New York:
  Harper and Row, 1980.
———. *Just War*. Milan: Edizioni Charta, 2005.

INDEX

~~~

ABOUT THE AUTHOR

E dward W. Wood, Jr. was born December 12, 1924 in Florence, Alabama. His youth was spent in a variety of places: the deep south of Mobile, Alabama, and the Gulf Coast, Charlotte, North Carolina, and the city of Chicago and its suburb, La Grange. At eighteen he volunteered for the draft in World War II and at nineteen for line duty out of an army college billet. Badly wounded by shrapnel in September 1944 in France, he received the Combat Infantryman's Badge, the Purple Heart, and the Bronze Star. During and after a difficult time of adjusting he received a PhB from the University of Chicago, a BA from Stanford University, a BLA from the University of Massachusetts, and a MCP from the Massachusetts Institute of Technology where he was a Sears Fellow in city planning. At the age of fifty-four he left city planning and started to write about issues of war and peace, violence and compassion in America. He has published two books—*On Being Wounded* and *Beyond the Weapons of our Fathers*—as well as articles in such periodicals as *War, Literature & the Arts,* Department of English and Fine Arts, United States Air Force Academy; *Friends Journal,* the Quaker monthly; and

Many Mountains Moving, the Boulder, Colorado, literary journal. He received three fellowships from the Wurlitzer Foundation in Taos, New Mexico, and won a national award for an essay on aging. He resides in Denver, Colorado and has three grown children.